The Cissells
of
Yakima and Ponoka

A Family History

David C. Cissell

Front cover. (Top) - Early map of Maryland (Nova Terrae-Mariae tabula), originally published 8 Sep 1635 in "*A Relation of Maryland*" a pamphlet intended to encourage colonists to come to Maryland. The map was engraved into the printing plate by Thomas Cecil. Thomas was likely a grandson of William Cecil, Lord Burghley; if so, he and the Cissell family share a common ancestor. (Bottom) - A view of Nerius Cissell's homestead near Ponoka, Alberta.

Rear Cover. (Background) - A view from the farm of William Victor Holden, near Yakima, WA. (Clockwise from lower left) - The author, ca. 1946 in Yakama, WA; Chad Cissell and Julie Zalikowski, in HI; The author and Judy Cissell Miller Jones, in Ponoka; Family house at 3414 Taylor Way; Space Shuttle and launch tower at Kennedy Space Center, near Cape Canaveral, FL.

Notations used:

    [ ] - Enclose Latitude, Longitude coordinates.

    { } - Enclose Author's personal comments or clarifications.

Sophie Scholl (9 May 1921 - 22 Feb 1943)

Table of Contents

Forward

This book documents the history of one branch of the Cissell family. It is centered on the family of Claud and Lois (Holden) Cissell, but includes many associated family branches and over 1000 individuals.

Much of the information was collected in bits and pieces while trying to determine the early origins of the family. It has been combined here in generally chronological order and to show the overall structure of the family.

This book is intended for two groups of people:

> The first and foremost are family members. I hope each will be able to see their context within the family and also, perhaps, within the broader scope of history itself.

> The second are family historians and genealogists. This book should provide a good road map to the family and so guide any specific research efforts one might have. Except where indicated, most of the information has come from publically available sources.

Detailed biographical information is provided for some individuals. General readers may well wish to skip over those sections. A few family secrets and personal notes have also been included.

Collecting and assembling this information has been very time consuming. I have to thank my wife, Julie Zalikowski, for her years of forbearance and support for this effort.

David Cissell
On the shore of Puget Sound, near Poulsbo
September 2014

Family Overview

The Cissell surname or some of its variants (Cecil, Cecyll, Seycell, Seyssel, Sissill, Sitsilt, etc.) have existed in England and Wales from at least the 1200's. One of the earliest members of that name known to have a direct connection with America was a Capt. William Cecil. He was on board the fleet commanded by Sir Francis Drake that left England in 1585 to attack Spanish settlements in America. The fleet stopped at Roanoke Island, but William did not survive the voyage[1]. There were also persons with various spellings of the surname in Virginia by the early 1600's, but none seem to have survived as families.

Most of the Cissell (& Cecil) families that have survived in North America came from three locations. The earliest, in the mid-1600's, was in St. Mary's County, Maryland mainly in the area around what is now Leonardtown, MD. These were Catholics, and most used the "Cissell" spelling. The second are found a short time later about 50 miles north in Prince George's County, MD. These were Protestants and used the spelling of "Cecil". The third arrived in the later part of the 1600's with William Penn in Philadelphia. They also used the "Cecil" spelling, and were initially, Quakers.

The connections between the three separate family groups and their English origins will be covered briefly in Chapter 12. This book, though, deals mostly with the Cissell's of St. Mary's County, MD.

---

[1] *Voyages of the Elizabethan Seamen to America*,1880, Ed. E. J. Payne, pg 254]

Maryland and St. Mary's County

In the late 1700's, a group of Cissell's and other families left St. Mary's County Maryland and moved to Pottinger's Creek[2], Kentucky, about 11 miles south of present day Bardstown. In the early 1800's some moved onto land provided by the Louisiana Purchase on the west side of the Mississippi river and were involved with the establishment of Perry County, Missouri. Following the Civil War, one family went north to Dodge County, Minnesota. In the late 1880's that family went west to what is now Oldham, Kingsbury County, South Dakota. In the early 1900's they moved to Ponoka, Alberta, Canada. Near the end of World War I, many family members returned to the United States and settled in Yakima, Washington.

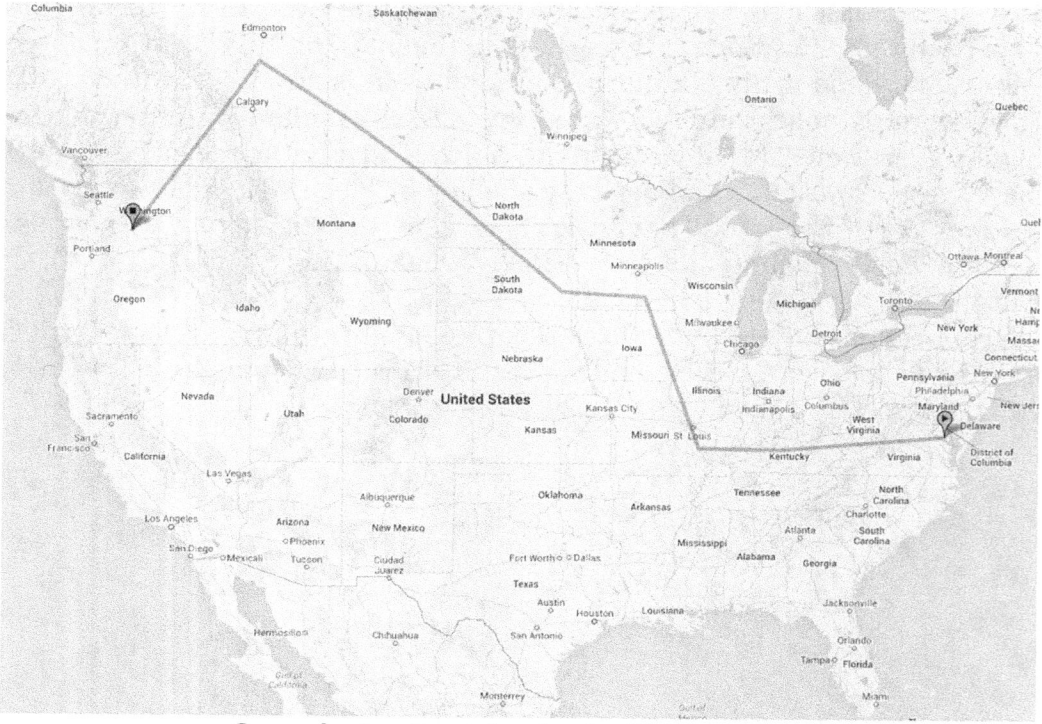

General migration taken by the family

The following chapters provide a history of these "Yakima and Ponoka" Cissells, their descendents, and selected related family lines.

---

[2] Latitude, Longitude location: [37.649633,-85.528988].

A number of people provided information for this book. Two that were especially helpful for the Ponoka Cissells were Emma Cissell Olmstead and Judy Cissell Miller Jones. An important individual for help with the initial and early American Cissell family research was Crolian William Edelen (1920-2006). The efforts of Timothy J. O'Rourke in documenting many of the St. Mary's County families, prior to his too early death, were also of important assistance.

x

1. Saint Mary's County, Maryland

The English settlement of what is now St. Mary's County Maryland began in 1634 with the arrival of Leonard Calvert, the first Governor of the Maryland Province, and about 120 other, mostly Catholic, colonists and sailors on board the Ark & the Dove. They landed first at St. Clement's Island and then, after buying about 30 miles of land from the Indians, began building the first town at what is now St. Mary's City.

There were no Cissells on those first two ships. The earliest record of a Cissell (Sissill) in Maryland is Rowland Sissill who appeared as a witness to two business agreements, the first on 1 March 1649 and another on 23 April 1649 [3]. No other records for Rowland have been found.

The next known record of the family in the Provence is found in land record patents[4] made on Tuesday, 21 June 1659 [5]. Two entries of interest were made that day and at apparently the same time as they are recorded one below the other:

> "John Shirtcliffe demands Land for the transportation of one Maid servant assigned by Robert Cole unto Mary and Ann Shertcliffe daughters of the said John. Rights Entered Aug[st] 15th 1657 folio 17. The said John likewise demands Land for the transportation of Tho[s] Spaulding the said John's Servant entered as aforesaid. Warrent for 100 acres of Land to the said John Shirtcliffe (ret.) the 25th of March next.
>
> John Cicill demands 50 Acres of Land for his own transportation in Anno 1658. Warrent inde return the 25th of March next."

This John Cicill is taken to be the founder of the St. Mary's County Cissell family and of the Yakima and Ponoka Cissells. This is due to his connections with John Shirtcliffe and the properties he was able to accumulate over his lifetime. It should be noted, however, that there was also a John Sissel who

---

[3] Maryland Historical Society, *Archives of Maryland, Judicial and Testamentary Business of the Provincial Court 1649/50-1657*, 1891, Ed. William Hand Brown, p 8.

[4] Persons who paid for the transportation of others to Maryland were granted 50 acres of land for each person they brought in. Persons who paid for their transportation (immigrated) to Maryland were also granted 50 acres of land.

[5] *Maryland State Archives, Land Office, Annapolis, Patents, Liber 4, folio 29 (Liber R)*

was transported into the Province by William Stevens (Stephens) in 1665 [6], but his history is not known.

John Shirtcliffe (Shercliffe) was older than John Cecill. He had been transported into the Province in 1638, but that name is also listed as an "immigrant" in 1646. Patent records connect him with the 100 Acre tract of land known as "Broad Neck" in St. Clement's Hundred as early as 1649; and which the Cissells would own in the next century. He had married Ann Spinke Goldsborough, sister of Henry Spinke, by 1647 and died 1663. In his will, which was written 1661 and probated March 1663, he mentions his wife, Anne; two sons, John and William; and two daughters, Mary and Anne. He also mentions his brother-in-law, Henry Spinke; this and other records leads many researchers to conclude that his wife was Henry's sister and that she had married a Goldsborough prior to coming to Maryland.

On 8 March 1831 a fire destroyed the county courthouse in Leonardtown, MD and many records were lost. Surviving documents include mostly land records and wills that had been previously copied and stored elsewhere. Accordingly, genealogy efforts in this area can be a challenge.

Two copies of John Cissell's will survive. It was written in 1694 and signed with a mark similar to a rough "I" or "J". A transcript of one copy [7] is provided here:

> In the name of God amen. The twenty eighth day of April, anno domini, one thousand six hundred, ninety four. I John Cissell of St. Marys County in the province of Maryland Planter, being sick and weak in body, but of Sound and perfect memory Thanks to the almighty god for the souls and calling to mind the uncertain state of this transitory life and that all flesh must yeld unto death, when it should please god to call and being desirous to settle things in order, doo make this my last will and testament, wherein is contained my last will & testament, in manner and form following. Revoking and absolutely unwillingly by these presents all and every testament or testaments, wills & wills, heretofore by me made, and be taken, only for my last will and testament and none other. First I bequeath my soul to almighty god, my maker and to Jesus Christ my redeemer, and to the holy ghost, my sanctifier, and my body to the earth from which it came, to be buried at Nutowne church, in such devout manner as my exect[rs] here after named shall be thought meet & convenient, item I give and Bequeath, unto my son John Cissell, fifty

---

[6] *Maryland State Archives Land Office, Annapolis, Liber 8, Folio 88.*
[7] Maryland Hall of Records, *Liber PC 1, pp 104-105. Also see Liber 7, Folio 382.*

acres of that parcel of land called by the name of Whit Acre, as it was formally divided by me. Item I give & bequeath unto Sonn William Cissell fifty Acres of that Parcel of Land called by the name of White acre as it was formally divided by me. Item I give & bequeath, unto my son Thomas Cissell fifty acres of that parcel of Land called by the name of White acre as it was formerly divided by me. Item My will is that the afore said hundred and fifty acres of Land, that is called by the name of White acre, I give it to my three sonns, John Cissill, William Cissill, and Thomas Cissill to them and their eirs forever. Item I give unto my two sonns Richard Cissill and Robert Cissill that parcel of land called by the name of Long necke containing one hundred acres to be equally divided between them two. to them and eros for ever, but in case either of my two sons should dey without issue, then the deceased part shall to my son James Cissill, to him & his eros forever. Item I give and bequeath unto my loving wife Mary Cissell this plantation which I now live on, during her life and after her decease, I bequeath it to my sonn Edward, Cissell to him & his eros forever, and in case my said sonn, should, before he comes to the age of one & twenty or without issue, then I bequeath it my youngest son, James Cissill, to him & his eros for ever. Item I give & bequeath unto my beloved wife Mary Cissill all the rest of my estate, to her proper use and (behoufe?). Item I do nominate appoint and constitute my beloved wife Mary Cissill whole & sole Executrix of my last will & testament. In witness of this my last will & testament I have here unto subscribed my and fixed my seal, the day and the year above ritten

John **I** {mark} Cissell {Seal}

Testis: John **R** {mark} Richards

Adam **✚** {mark} Head

Mary **O** {mark} Mekin
Robert Asiter {no mark indicated}

A probate certification statement was also included at the end of the copied will:

"June ye 6th 1698
Then did Addam Head (,) Robert Asitor, two of the to the (sic) Wtts in writing dispose (uppon?) their oath, that they heared the same read, unto the testator & that he did approve the Same, & did,

> thereupon Signe, Seale & deliver, the same as his last will &
> testament and that at the time thereof, he was of Sound disposing
> mind, to the best of their judgment and further the above witnesses
> did depose, that they see Mary Meackins signe the said writing as
> witness to the same."

Given that John Cissell did not sign his will but instead just made his mark
and given that the will had to be read to him for his approval, it is clear that
he was not literate.

On 26 Jul 1698 an inventory of John Cissell's personal effects was made and
showed an appraised value of £75/11/- [8].   Among the items listed was a
"parcel of old books"; this is interesting given that John was not literate. The
estate inventory [9] for his son, Thomas, also included old books, but it is not
known if they were the same books or how either may have been related to
earlier Cissell generations.

Except for land and probate records, few documents related to John Cissell
remain. Those that survive include:

> In 1661, John Cessell made oath [10] before the Provincial Court
> held at St. Mary's that Richard Bennett refused to assist
> Thomas Bassett, constable of New Towne Hundred, in his
> duties of carrying Robert Ford before Colonel William Evans,
> one of the Justices of the Peace for St. Mary's County. He made
> his mark with a crossed "I" similar to: ł.

> In 1679, he served as a member of a jury at the Provincial
> Court during lawsuits over the estate of Colonel William Evans,
> deceased [11].

and,

> In 1697/8 at session of the council, a John Cissle was paid £8
> "for fixing arms according to the order of the council" [12]. This
> is often taken to mean that John Cissell was a gunsmith.
> However, given that this was just a few months prior to his

---

[8] Maryland Hall of records, Inventories & Accounts, Liber 16, folio 200.

[9] Maryland Hall of Records, Inventories & Accounts, Liber 10, folio 143.

[10] *Archives of Maryland, Vol. 41*, p. 553.

[11] *Archives of Maryland, Vol. 51*, pp. 282-285.

[12] *Archives of Maryland, Vol. 23*, p. 366.

death and that the council record does not identify which "John Cissle" out of the several[13] then in the Province, this attribution may well be incorrect.

As indicated by his will and associated land records, John Cissell owned about 500 acres of land at his death. His will identifies him as a planter (farmer). A major cash crop at that time was tobacco, and given the size of his land holdings, it is likely that he did grow that crop.

His will did not identify his dwelling plantation, but it is generally taken to have been "Poplar Neck". This was a freehold of 200 acres lying in New Towne Hundred[14] that had originally been surveyed for William Brough on 25 November 1642.

One of the land tracts mentioned in the will was "White Acre". This was a free hold of 150 acres lying on the West side of Bretton Bay. This was surveyed for Samuel Harris on 12 November 1652 and was sold by him to William Bradley. It was patented by Bradley on 7 August 1658 and then assigned by him to Christopher Goodacre.

Another tract was "Long Acre". This was of 100 acres of land and located in New Towne Hundred "by a small cut of Devil's back creek".

Edward Cissell who was supposed to inherit the dwelling plantation appears to have died without issue before 1707. In that year he owned no land in St. Mary's County and the plantation of "Poplar Neck" of 200 acres was allocated as follows [15]: W[m] Cecill 25 acres, James Cecill 25 acres, Thomas Cecill 50 acres, Mary Dant [16] 50 acres, and Tho[s] Cecill 50 acres.

---

[13] Including his own son, John, and a John Cecil in Prince George's County.

[14] St. Mary's County was divided into 10 smaller administrative divisions called Hundreds. The three that were most relevance for the Cissell families were New Towne Hundred, centered on what is now Leonardtown, MD; St. Clement's Hundred, joining on its West; and Poplar Hill Hundred, joining on the East. All are bounded on the South by the Potomac River.

[15] Maryland Hall of Records, Rent Rolls 7&8 (1&2), folio 24. For a printed abstract also see: *St. Mary's County Maryland, Rent Rolls, 1639-1771*, T.L.C. Genealogy, 1993, pg 27.

[16] Given that John Cissell's will mentioned no daughters, this Mary is often taken to have been his widow and who had married a Dant after John's death.

A plot of these tracts near Leonardtown and Compton, MD is shown here [17]:

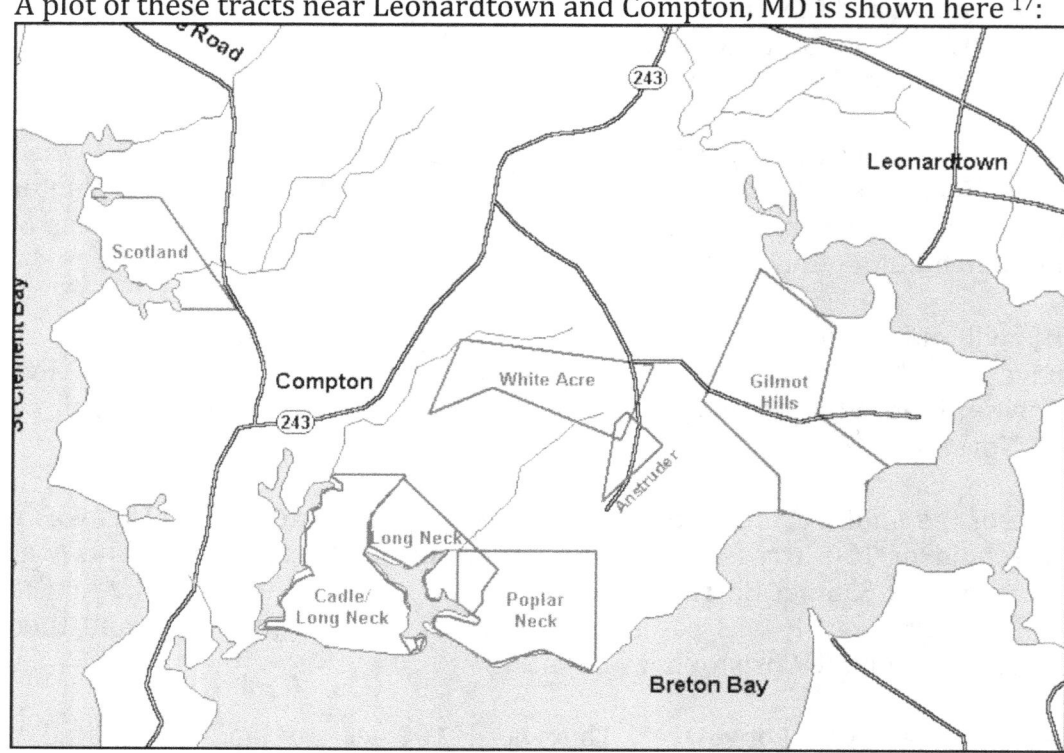

The listing of "Thomas Cecil" twice in the rent roll is of some interest in that it could suggest that there may have been two closely related Thomas Cecil's. A "Tho. Sissell" was listed as one of 14 persons transported into the Province in 1675 by John Stevenson [18]. This Thomas Sissell married Mary, the widow of Robert Thompson sometime after 1 November 1697[19]. His marriage was brief though, in that his will was dated 18 October 1700 and submitted to probate on 28 March 1701. The will mentions an "unborn child" and an unnamed plantation of 100 acres. It mentions no Cissell's and none served as witnesses to the will or to any of the probate records. It is assumed therefore, that this Thomas Sissell was not related closely to those associated with "Poplar Neck". His connection with the John Cissell family remains unknown.

The identity of John Cissell's wife, Mary, has been a subject of conjecture and much work since at least the early 1900s. It has been suggested that she may

---

[17] St. Mary's County Historical Society, Peter Himmelheber.

[18] Maryland Hall of Records, Patents, Liber 15, Folio 353.

[19] Maryland Hall of records, Inventories & Accounts, Liber 15, folio 215.

have been Mary Calvert, but a review [20], by the genealogist Harry Newman, of the Calvert family could not fit her into that family in this time period and he could find no other records to support this suggestion. Another suggestion, made by Newman and others, is that John Cissell's wife was Mary Shirtcliffe, the daughter of John Shirtcliffe and that after John Cissell's death she married John Dant [21], one of the witnesses to the will of John Shirtcliffe. This is based in part on a rent roll that listed "Mary Dant" as possessing 50 Acres of Poplar Neck and the assumption that this was his wife. Given that John Cissell lived near the Shirtcliffe's and that they had known each other at least as early as John's application for land in 1659, this suggestion is not unreasonable and deserves some examination.

On 22 November, 1712 depositions were taken as part of a lawsuit over land that had been sold by John Nunn to John Shirtcliffe and Henry Spinke. One of the dependents was identified as Mary Dent (possibly Dant) and a daughter of John Schertilife (Shirtcliffe):

" John Dansey's Dep.[s] about Land

Maryland fs S.[t] Marys County November y.[e] 22.[d] 1712

In Pursuance to a Comission out of the honble High Court of Chancery for the Province afd to us underneath written bearing date the 11.th die Octob.[r] 1712   In obedience to the said Comission according have Mett on the Land in the possession of John Dansey Esq formerly Escheated and some time in the possession of John Mann having called what Evidences the said John Dansey Esq Desired and haveing taken their Corporall oaths upon the holy Evangelists on the said Land declare as followeth

The Deposition of John Fosieg Aged seventy three years or thereabouts Having taken his oath on the holy Evangelist and doth Declare that John Bayley sold John Warren about thirty five or thirty six years agoe but seventy five Acres of Land and that the said John Warren lived upon one hundred and fifty Acres of Land which was then made Escheatable to my Lord Baltemore which was the Land that John Nunn sold to John Shattelef and Henry Spink And this Deponent further ~~saith~~ Declareth that he has heard Augustinian Warren the son of John Warren often say that the Peir Tree now

[20] College of Southern Maryland Studies Center, Harry Wright Newman Collection, Subseries: Cecil, Box Number: 16, 1978.

[21] College of Southern Maryland Studies Center, Harry Wright Newman Collection, Subseries: Cecil, Box Number: 16, 1978

standing was the bounds betwixt John Bayley and his father and that the said Peir Tree stands within forty or fifty yards of the said Valley which is Esteemed the bounds of said Land And this Depon.^t further saith that he has heard old John Warren say that the popler which he saw green now dead the same to be seen is the bound Tree betwixt the said John Bayley and John Warren and further saith that the said John Bayley Tendered the said Depon.^t the whole Tract of Land he had which was then intire but one hundred & fifty Acres And the Depon.^t further saith that the said Bayley never had any pretentions to the Land which was formerly Nunns Land sold from the said John to John Shattelof & Henry Spinck
and furth saith not

The Deposition of Mrs Mary Dent Aged sixty five years or thereabouts being sworne on the hold Evangelist and doth declare That her father John Schertilife her mother Anne Schertilife her Uncle Henry Spinck often ~~times~~ say that her said father and Uncle sold the Tract of Land beginning in the Valley where there was a well about fifty or sixty yards from her father then dwelling house to Edward Cotten And this Depon.^t further saith when her father and mother lived on the said Land there was a Chaple some Distance from her fathers house about one hundred and fifty yards or thereabouts

This Depon.^t further saith that she heard her father and Mother say when they sold the said Land to Edward Cotten that there was a reservation made of tenn apple trees between the house then standing and the waterside which soon after the said Edward Cotten dyed so they lost their Priviledge of removeing the said apple trees by John Warren who Entred upon the said Land and further saith not

Wittness our hands & seales the day & year above written
Gerard Slye (S)
Wm Watts (S)"

Could this Mary (the daughter of John Shirtcliffe) have been the Mary Dant listed on the rent roll for Poplar Neck, and could she have been John Cissell's wife?

Mary Shirtcliffe certainly did marry Peter Mills:

On 24 April 1667,
> "came Peter Mills and demands land by virtue of his marriage with Mary the daughter of John Sherclife. Warrent then issue in the name of Peter Mills for 100 acres of land due to him by marriage with Mary the daughter of John Sherclife and by the said Sherclife bequeathed to the said Mary being due to him for transporting Josephat Dorrell and Elizabeth Morgan" [22].

Peter Mills and Mary had three Children: Elizabeth who married first William Spink and then Charles Daft; Nicholas who married Elizabeth Heard; and Peter who married Frances Slye. Mary's husband, Peter, died in 1684.

If this Mary Shirtcliffe had been the only wife of John Cissell, then the following chronology would apply:

~1638 - John Cissell born.

1647 - Mary Shirtcliffe born.

1663 - John Shirtcliffe died. Mary age 16.

1664-1667 - Peter Mills marries Mary Shirtcliffe. Mary age 17-20.

1685 - Peter Mills dies. 18-21 years of marriage. Mary age 38.

~1686 - John Cissell marries Mary Shirtcliffe Mills. John age ~48; Mary age ~39. The eldest Cissell son, John, would then have been born about 1687. The youngest son, James, could not have been born before about 1693.

1698 - John Cissell dies, age ~60. 12 years of marriage & at least 7 children. Mary age 51.

1698+ - Mary Shirtcliffe Mills Cissell marries ____ Dant.

---

[22] Maryland Hall of Records, Liber 10, Folio 477

It seems unlikely that John Cissell would have been able to farm on his own for 27 years (from 1659 to 1686) without a family and then have 7 children starting at age 48.

Another way to consider the rent roll information for Poplar Neck is to assume that the Mary listed was not the wife of John Cissell, but that she was the wife of one of his sons or even, possibly, his daughter. John's wife Mary did not administer the estate as the will had requested. Instead John (apparent the eldest son) did this; his sureties being Thomas Dant and Henry Spink. This might suggest that John's wife had died perhaps in 1698 or earlier.

Similarly, the will would have had Mary or Edward or James owning all of Poplar Neck, depending on who died and when. (When Mary died it was to go to Edward; if Edward died (before age 21 or without issue), the plantation was to go to the youngest son, James.) But the rent roll shows that the tract was not allocated in that manner. Poplar Neck seems to have been broken into four 50-Acre sections and then one of those was further broken into two 25 Acre pieces. Of the 50 Acre sections, Thomas had two and Mary one. This would suggest that John Cissell's desires, made in 1694, could not be complied with for some reason. By 1707 it seems likely that at least Richard, Robert, and Edward had died (most likely) or moved from the area. Surviving records do not define when they may have died, if they had married, or how the family allocated property in response to their individual losses.

The identity of John Cissell's wife, then, remains unknown and will likely require information from sources other than the surviving paper records for an answer.

In any event, the children of John Cissell and Mary were:

1. John Cissell. Died ca. 1722 in St. Mary's County with no known wife or children.

2. William Cissell. Died ca 1744 in St. Mary's County. Married Catherine Joyner (born by 1669, died -by 1714), daughter of Robert Joyner [23]. Will was written 22 Jun 1742 and probated 1744. Children included:

> 2-1. John. Died by 1742. Wife was Elizabeth who married secondly Charles Neale. Child was William.

---

[23] Will of Robert Joyner. Md. Cal. Wills, Vol 1, p.71 and Wills, Liber 1, folio 512

2-2. Arthur. Died ca. 1750. Wife was Mary ___. Children included John, Elinor, Margaret, Ann, Monica, and James.

2-3. Luke. Died ca.1747. Died poor and may have had a son named Luke.

2-4. Margaret married John Thompson.

2-5. Ann Edwards

2-6. Matthew. Died 1748. Wife Mary (Payne?). Child was Charles.

2-7. Elizabeth. Married Charles Payne.

2-8? Clare. Married ___ Barton. Listed as "daughter" in William's will, but she may have been a great daughter-in-law.

3. Thomas Cissell. Died 1724 in St. Mary's County. Wife was Frances. Children included:

> 3-1. John. Born est. 1690, Died 1743 in St. Mary's County. Wife Sarah. Children included Thomas, John, and Mary Ann.

> 3-2. James. Born by 1724.

4. Richard Cissell. Born by 1694.

5. Robert Cissell. Born by 1694.

6. Edward Cissell. Born by 1694.

7. James Cissell. Born by 1694. Died Mar/Apr 1717 in St. Mary's County. Ancestor of the Yakima and Ponoka Cissells.

The Will of James Cissell was written 30 Mar 1717 and proved 22 Apr 1717 [24]:

> "In the Name of god amen. I James Cissell of St. Mary's County being week of body but of sound and perfect memory and considering the uncertainty of this transitory Life I do think it fit and convenient to make this my last Will and Testament. Renouncing revoking and making void all other Wills heretofore by me made or intended to be made either verbal or in writing and I do appoint this to be my last Will & Testament.
>
> Item First: and principally I bequeath my soul to almighty god my Savoir and Redeemer by who's meritorious Death and passion I hope

---

[24] Maryland Hall of Records, Wills, Liber 14, folio 339. Minor spelling changes made for clarity.

to have full pardon and absolution of all my past crimes & sins and my body to be decently buried at the Discretion of my Execut^r hereafter mentioned and appointed. And for what worldly Estate it hath pleased almighty god of his goodness to bless me with and after my just debts are paid I dispose of them in manner and forms following.

2^{ly} Item: I give and bequeath onto my beloved son James Cissell and to his heirs forever my plantation that I now live on with twenty five acres of land known by the name of Poplar Neck as also fifty acres of land being the moiety of one hundred acres of Land called by the name of Broadneck wch s^d fifty acres or moiety of Land I give and bequeath unto my s^d Son James Cissell and his heirs forever.

3^{ly} Item: I give unto my beloved Daughters Mary & Ruth Cissell and to their heirs for ever the other fifty acres or moiety of Land called Broadneck to be Equally divided unto my said two Daughters Mary and Ruth Cissell and to their heirs for ever and if it pleases god either of my said Daughters dies before they come of age or without lawful heir that then the whole fifty acres or moiety of Land to the survivor and her heirs for ever.

4^{thly} Item: I give and bequeath unto my Son James Cissell my best bed and furniture to it belonging.

5^{ly} Item: I give unto my Daughter Mary Cissell the bed I now lie upon with the furniture to it belonging.

6^{ly} Item: I give and bequeath all the remainder part of my Estate (as well ___as dead?) to be Equally Divided between my three Children James, Mary, & Ruth Cissell & if it pleases god either of my s^d Children before named Shall dye in their minority or (marriage?) that then their part be Equally divided to the Survivors accordingly as is within Expressed not altering the property of Mary & Ruth's moiety on fifty acres of Land as is before expressed.

7^{ly} & Lastly Item: and for the fulfilling, Executing and effecting of this my last Will and Testament, I appoint my (grantee?) and well loved friend Charles Neale to be whole and sole Executor of this my last Will & Testament. In witness where of I have here unto set my hand and seal this Thirtyth Day of March 1717.

James ^{his}O_{mark} Cissell {Seal}

Sealed signed and delivered in the presence of

John [his]+[mark] Brown, Margaret [her]+[mark]Anderson, Clair [her]O[mark] Moore, James Thompson

And at the end of the foregoing will was thus written viz[t]:

Then comes John Brown, Clair Moore and James Thompson three of the witnesses to the above Will and made oath that they saw the above named James Cissell seal sign and deliver the same as his last Will and Testament

Wm Aisquith...."

Since James signed his will by making his mark, and not by actual signature, it is clear that he, like his father, was not literate. The wife of James is sometimes identified as Mary, but no mention of her is made in his will and so this should be treated with caution. The children of James are identified and were:

7-1. James Cissell. Born by 1717 in St. Mary's County. Died 1785. James is an ancestor of the Yakima and Ponoka Cissells. His wife was Mary. The children of James and Mary included:

> 7-1-1. Ignatius Cissell. Born 1724 in St. Mary's County. Died 1788 in Nelson Co., KY. Wife Elizabeth. Ancestor of the Bluffton, Alberta Cissells[25]. Children included Edmond Barton Cissell, James Rodolph "Rhody" Cissell, Ignatius Cissell, Jr., Joseph Cissell, James Cissell, Mary Cissell, Wilford Cissell, Eleanor Cissell, and Bennett Cissell.

> 7-1-2. Francis Cissell. Married Winfred Berryman on 19 Aug 1808 in Nelson Co., KY.

> 7-1-3. Bennett Cissell. Born in St. Mary's County and probably died in Washington Co., KY.

> 7-1-4. **Bernard Cissell**. Born 12 (or 15) Feb 1759 in St. Mary's County[26]. Died 4 Jul 1833 Perry Co., MO. Bernard is an ancestor of the Yakima and Ponoka Cissells. Wife Monica Payne (13 Mar 1763 - 3 Feb 1837), daughter of Leonard and Monica

---

[25] See Chapter 11.

[26] Records of St. Andrew's Episcopal Church, Leonardtown, MD.

Cissell Payne[27]. Bernard and Monica are both buried in Mount Hope Cemetery, Perryville, MO[28]. (More information later.)

7-1-5. Susanna Cissell. Born 28 Jan 1760 in St. Mary's County. Married Raphael Wimsatt ca 1783.

71-6. Peter Cissell. Born 29 Jun 1764. Died ca 1803 Washington, CO., KY. Wife Eleanor.

71-7. Rachel Cissell. Living in Newtown, St. Mary's County in 1785.

71-8. Anastasia Cissell.

71-9 Rebecca Cissell.

7-2. Mary Cissell. Nothing known

7-3. Ruth Cissell. Nothing known.

Maryland had been started by the Catholic Calvert family as a province offering religious freedom. Many Catholics, including John Cissell, had come there in part for that reason. William Bretton patented 750 acres on Newtown Neck in 1640 and later that year the Jesuits established a mission there. (Church ownership of the land lasted until 2009 when it was sold to the State of Maryland.)

Political turmoil in England in the 1640s through the 1650s required the Jesuits and their Catholic members to keep a low profile. Establishment of a large church building would not have been wise, but a small chapel was of less risk. In 1661 William Bretton donated [29] an acre and a half of his land for such a chapel and for a graveyard for the Catholics; the chapel was built the following year:

---

[27] Monica Cissell, the wife of Leonard Payne was the daughter of Arthur Cissell and Mary Doyne; the grand daughter of William Cissell and Catherine Joyner; and thus the great-grand daughter of John Cissell. Since Bernard was the grandson of this same John Cissell, his wife, Monica Payne (the gg-grand daughter of John Cissell), was his 1st cousin, 2 times removed.

[28] Monica is in Row 17, Stone 11.

[29] Maryland Hall of Records, Liber PCR, folio 1026 (April the 12th 1662) and *Archives of Maryland, XLI, Proceedings of the Provincial Court of Maryland 1658-1662*, Ed. Bernard Christian Steiner, 1922, p. 531.

"This day came Mr William Bretton and desired the ensueing to be recorded (vizt)

Ad perpetuam rei memoriam

Forasmuch as divers good and Zealous Roman Catholick Inhabitants of New Towne and St Clements Bay have unanimously agreed amongst themselves to erect and build a Church or Chappell whether they may repayre on Sundays and other Holy dayes appoynted and Cormanded by holy Church to serue Almighty God and heare divine Service, And the most Convenient place for that purpose desired and pitcht upon by them all, is on a certaine parcell of the Land belonging to William Bretton, Gent Now Knowe yee that I William Bretton of Little Bretton in the County of St Marys in the Province of Maryland gent, with the hearty good likeing of my dearly beloued wife Temperance Bretton, To the greater hono^r and Glory of Almighty God the euer immaculat Virgin Mary and all Saints haue given and doe hereby freely & for euer give to the behoofe of the said Roman Catholick Inhabitants and their Posterity or Successors Roman Catholicks soe much land as they shall build the said Church or Chappell on which for their better Convenience they may frequent to serue Almighty God and heare divine Service as aforesaid with such other land adjoyning to the said Church or Chappel convenient Likewise for a Church yard wherein to bury their dead Conteyning ab^t one acre and halfe of Ground Scituate and lying on a devident of land called Brettons Out Lett, and on the Easte side of the said devident neere to the head of a Creeke called St Williams Creeke which falleth into St Nicholas Creeke and neare unto the narrowest place of the freehould of Little Brittaine.

Tenth day of November Anno domini 1661 Wm Bretton, Temperance Bretton

Delivered and Signed and Sealed in the p^rsence of Wm Evans James Thompson Luke Gardner Robert Cole "

John Cissell, in his will, had asked to be buried at this Newtown Cemetery and his family would have complied with his wishes. At that time it would not have been unusual for family members to be buried on their farm or plantation, but given the presence of such a close Catholic cemetery (about 1.4 miles from Poplar Neck), it is likely that many of the other Cissell family members are buried there as well.

The Newtown Church (St. Ignatius) was one of the first English Speaking Catholic churches established in North America. Its cemetery has operated continuously since 1662 with only a name change to St. Francis Xavier. A replacement church was built ca. 1731 about 0.5 miles South of the cemetery.

The cemetery[30] may well be the oldest of its type in the United States. Unfortunately no records of the early burial sites were made. No head stones for any of the Cissell family members have survived and their actual burial locations in the cemetery are not currently known.

Newtown (St. Francis Xavier) Cemetery

---

[30] latitude, longitude: [38.263235, -76.6977]

2. Pottinger's Creek and Kentucky

By the time of Bernard Cissell, the conclusion of the Revolutionary War brought change to St. Mary's County. The need for supplies for the war and the subsequent halt of trade with England lead to a decline in the economy there. Confiscation of previous British property also caused loss of land to many of the resident families. At the same time vast new expanses of land became available west of the Appalachian mountains and could be purchased at low cost. Because of this, and the continuing difficulties in being able to practice their religion, a group of about 60 families from the Maryland counties of St. Mary's, Charles, and Prince George's, formed a "Catholic League of Families" in 1785. They pledged to migrate to Kentucky; not all at once, but as each was able to do so.

The first group of 25 families, mostly from St. Mary's County, left Maryland in 1785 under the leadership of Basil Hayden for Pottinger's Creek in Nelson County, KY. Their route [31] started overland to Pittsburgh, and then in flatboats down the Ohio River to Maysville. This landing was chosen because the country downstream, bordering on the river above present day Louisville (the Falls of the Ohio), was known to be subject to attacks by Indians. They then marched overland from Maysville down to a fort at Goodwin's Station (near the present Boston, KY). This was the nearest fortified post to their prearranged destination lands at Pottinger's Creek. From there they moved into the Pottinger's Creek area of Nelson County about 12 or 15 miles Southeast of the station, near the present day town of Holy Cross.

Bernard Cissell was part of the group to settle at Pottinger's Creek. The group included [32]:

> Basil Hayden, Philip Lee, William Bald, Bernard Cissell, Charles Payne, William Brewer, Leonard Johnson, Henry McAtee, Joseph Clark, Stephen Elliott, James Mollihorne, Henry Norris, Ignatius Cissell, Ignatius Byrne, Randal Hagan, Ignatius Hagan, Jeremiah Brown, Robert Cissell, Ignatius Bowles, Hezekiah

---

[31] *The Centenary of Catholicity in Kentucky*, 1884, Ben. J. Webb, pp. 27-28.
[32] *The Centenary of Catholicity in Kentucky*, 1884, Ben. J. Webb, p. 28.

Luckett, Stanislaus Melton, Thomas Bowlin, John Baptist Dant, Philip Miles, Harry Hill, John Hutchins, Isaac Thawles, John Spalding, William Mahony, Henry Lucas, William Bowles, John Bowles, James Queen, Bernard Nally, James Stevens, Ignatius French, Washington Boone, Francis Bryan, Jeremiah Wathen, Thomas Mudd, Raphael R. Mudd, Walter Burch, Philip Mattingly, Joseph Spalding, James Dant, Joseph Dant, Urban Speaks, Joseph Edelin, Joseph Howe, Joseph Mills, Harry Miles, Monica Hagan, Rodolphus Norris, Francis Peak.

William Bald, Bernard Cissell, Charles Payne and William Brewer formed the first board of trustees organized in Kentucky for the secure tenure of Catholic Church property. The deed of transfer of the grounds attached to Holy Cross Church, the first erected in the State, reads as follows [33]:

"This indenture, made this first day of May, in the year of our Lord, 1798, between Basil Hayden, Sr., of the county of Washington and State of Kentucky, on the one part, and William Bald, Bernard Cissell, Charles Payne and William Brewer, of the county and State aforesaid, of the other part, witnesseth : That the said Basil Hayden, for and in consideration of the sum of five pounds, good, lawful and current money of Kentucky, to him in hand paid by the said William Bald, Bernard Cissell, Charles Payne and William Brewer, the receipt whereof I do hereby acknowledge, and thereof do release and acquit them, the said William Bald, Bernard Cissell, Charles Payne, and William Brewer, their heirs, executors and administrators: I, the said Basil Hayden, hath this day granted, bargained and sold unto the said William Bald, Bernard Cissell, Charles Payne and William Brewer, their heirs, executors and administrators, for the use of the Roman Catholic Church forever, a certain tract or parcel of land containing two acres, more or less, situated, lying and being in the county of, Washington, and on the waters of Pottinger's creek, including the chapel in the centre, and bounded as follows: Beginning at a hickory standing 45" W., twelve and a half poles from said chapel, running thence due east eight poles to a white oak sapling ; thence due south eighteen poles to a white oak and hickory ; thence due west eighteen poles to a dogwood ; thence due north eighteen poles to the beginning ; and all the appurtenances there- unto belonging ; to have and to hold the said two acres of land, to the said William Bald, Bernard Cissell, Charles Payne and William Brewer, for the only purpose and benefit of the Roman Catholic Church ; and I, the said Basil Hayden, Sr., for myself and my heirs, unto the said William

---

[33] *The Centenary of Catholicity in Kentucky*, 1884, Ben. J. Webb, p. 29.

Bald, Bernard Cissell, Charles Payne and William Brewer, and their heirs, do the said land and premises from my heirs and all and every person claiming by or under us, warrant and forever defend. In testimony, etc. Basil Hayden."

"Attest: John Reed, Clerk."

Bernard Cissell remained at Pottinger's Creek until 1803. Today, the family is remembered somewhat by a road called "Cissell Lane", just off highway 457 Southwest of Holy Cross, and by the family burials in the cemetery of the Holy Cross church that Bernard had helped start.

3. Perry County, Missouri

In 1803, at about the time of the Louisiana Purchase by the United States from France, Bernard and his family left Kentucky and moved to a place about 5 miles West of the Mississippi River into what is now Missouri, [34]. In 1806, he made a claim to the United States for the land that he had settled on [35]:

> "Bernard Cecil, claiming eight hundred and ninety-four arpends [36] of land, situate on Saline creek, district of St. Genevieve; produces a certificate of permission to settle from Pierre Deluziere, commandant, dated 14th December, 1805; a plat of survey, certified 5th February, 1806.
>
> Testimony taken, April 1st, 1806. Clement Haydon, being duly sworn, says that claimant had, on the 20th December, 1803, a wife and four children; that he was then preparing to build a house on said land; that in 1804 he raised a crop on the same, and has actually inhabited and cultivated it to this day; that prior to claimant moving on said land, there was a house on what he intended to survey; but that one Hawkins, in surveying the adjoining tract, had surveyed the same; and further, that the family of said claimant, was in the said year 1803, all sick, and thereby had not it their power to cultivate the said tract.
>
> April 23d, 1810: Present, Lucas and Penrose, commissioners. It is the opinion of the Board that his claim ought not to be granted."

Although his claim was not accepted on this first attempt, a 640-acre portion was eventually approved [37]. His claim was located on the South fork of Saline Creek between the claims of John Hawking, a principle surveyor in the area, and Henry Graf. This is an area a little NW of the current town of Perryville, MO[38]. The creek got its name from a salt springs. The French, and then the Americans, would boil and evaporate

---

[34] A History of Missouri, Volume I, 1908, Louis Houck, pg. 384.

[35] American State Papers, Volume II, from March 4th 1789 to February 27th, 1809, 1834, Ed. Walter Lowrie, pg 423.

[36] A French measure of land. In Missouri, an arpend was equal to about 0.8507 acres.

[37] American State Papers, Volume III., from December 22, 1815 to May 26, 1824, 1834, Ed. Walter Lowrie, pg 308.

[38] The author has a direct connection to Perryville in that the architectural design for his home was from a contemporary resident there, Rocio Romero.

the water leaving the salt behind. Most of the salt was then taken to New Orleans for sale.

Bernard and Monica had four children:

1. Lewis Cissell. Born ca. 1784 in St. Mary's County, MD. Buried 7 Jun 1858, Perry County, MO. Married Anna Maria Mattingly 28 Jun 1814 in Washington County, KY. They had the following children: Ann Mahala; Joseph; Sarah; Bernard; Isabella; Augustine; Cecilia; Martina; Gabriel; Elizabeth Philomena; Mary Jane; Victoria Ferdinanda; Mary Ann; and Mary Jane.

2. Mary J. (Poly) Cissell. Born ca. 1786 in Kentucky. Died 11(9?) Jul 1835, Perry County, MO. Married Simon Duvall (son of John Miles Duval and Anne Arpy Tarleton) on 31 Jan 1804, Ste. Genevieve, MO.   Children included: Lewis/Louis; Sarah; Mary; Elizabeth; Theresa; Joseph; Simon C.; Clement S.; John Chrysostom; Ann Arpy (Lucy); Rosa(lia); and Thomas P.S.

3. Clement Cissell. Born 15 Oct 1789 in Kentucky. Died 15 May 1859, Perry County, MO. Married Anne Layton (daughter of Joseph Layton and Mary Ann Downs) 25 Sep 1810 in Perry County, MO. Children included: Mary; Elizabeth; Catherine; Theresa; Leo; Mary Ann; Helena; Isidore; Francis; and Hillary.

4. **Joseph Cissell**. Born Jan 22 1792 in Kentucky. Died 22 Mar 1878, Perry County, MO. Married first (Mary) Ann Miles (Daughter of Joseph Miles and Anne Wathen) ca. 1816 in Perry County, MO. Ann was born 5 Apr 1795 in Kentucky and died two days before Christmas 1825, possibly as a result of an accident [39].   Joseph and Ann are both buried in the Mount Hope Cemetery, Perryville, MO. Ann left the following children:

> 4-1. Mary Martina Cissell (ca 1817- after 1880) who married Raymond Tucker, son of Peter Tucker and Christina Hagan.

> 4-2. **Narius Cissell**, born ca 1819 (Continued)

> 4-3. Vincent Cissell, born 15 Oct 1821. Died 20 Mar 1903, Perry County, MO. Married Mary Caroline French (Daughter of Lewis French and Mary Manning) 23 Feb 1846, Perryville, MO. Children included: Leo Ferdinand (1847-1851); Mary Lavinia (16 Aug 1849- 21 May 1922); Victoria Anna (9 Aug 1851- 17 Feb 1925); Mary Ann

---

[39] History of Southeast Missouri, 1888, Godspeed Publishing Company, pp. 693-694.

(16 Sep 1853-10 Nov 1918); Celestian Albert (1 Oct 1857-29 Jan 1927); and Anna Ambrosia (3 Mar 1860-25 May 1965).

4-4.   Lewis, born 20 Jul 1823. Died 13 Apr 1892, St. Mary, MO. Married Louisa Jane Mattingly (daughter of James Mattingly and Ann Manning) 24 Nov 1846 in Perryville, MO. Children included: John Verius(Veris) (ca 17 Aug 1847-9 Dec 1891) [40]; Ann Loretta (4 Jan 1849-   ); Leo Ferdinand (7 Mar 1852-23 Nov 1901); Mary Teresa (2 Oct 1853- 12 Mar 1867); Joseph Emmanuel (12 Apr 1855(6)-11 Jan 1916); Ezekiel (11 May 1857-19 Jan 1893); Mary Jane Frances (12 Jun 1859-2 Feb 1939); Lewis Kenrick(Kendrick) (24 Feb 1861-23 Oct 1928); Henry Pius (16 Dec 1862-Mar 1867); Mary Louisa (30 Apr 1865- Nov 1865); Vincent (3 Feb 1868-18 Dec 1942); and William Aloysius (23 Jan 1870-1939)

and,

 4-5.   Henry Pius Cissell, born 31 Mar 1825. Died 10 Jan 1877. Married Christina Miles (daughter of Francis Miles and Christina Tucker) 2 Sep 1845 in Perryville, MO. Children included: Mary Anastasia (30 Jan 1851-1 Aug 1921); Vincent (3 Sep 1852-   ); Joseph Francis (1 Sep 1854-20 Mar 1877); John Arcinius (bpt. 24 Feb 1857 age 2 mos. - Bur 20 Oct 1865); Mary Christina (29 Dec 1858 - 1921); Francis Xavier (9 Nov 1860-20 Mar 1877); and Henry Pius, Jr. (27 Apr 1863-).

Joseph married secondly, Mary (Manning) Warren (daughter of James Manning and Elizabeth Riley and widow of Michael Warren) on 27 Apr 1835 in Perryville, MO. Children included:

4-6.   Leo Cissell born 10 Apr 1836 and died 4 Mar 1842, Perry County, MO.;

4-7.   Henry Angelo Cissell, born Jul 1838, died 27 Dec 1838, Perry County, MO.;

4-8.   Joseph Clement Cissell, born 15 Apr 1840, died 19 Sep 1872 Perry County, MO. Married Rosalie Philomena Duvall (Daughter of Simeon Duvall and Mary Miles) 21 Oct 1861 in Perryville, MO.

---

[40] A grandson of John Verius Cissell, named Chalmer William (Chip) Cissell (3 Jan 1904-15 Mar 1949), was once a baseball short-stop for the Chicago White Sox. He also played for Portland, the Cleveland Indians, Boston Red Sox, Philadelphia Athletics, New York Giants and Baltimore (in the old International League). He died, however, in poverty.

Children included: Henry Leo (6 Nov 1866-2 Sep 1872); Edwina Maria (bpt. 26 Jan 1868) [41]; John Leonard (26 Jan 1870 -   ); and James Matthew (Maddison) (12 Feb 1872-19 Aug 1937);

4-9.   Leo Cissell born 14 May 1842, died 25 Nov 1861 Perry County, MO.;

4-10.   Mary Ann Cissell Born ca. 1845, died 11 Mar 1922, Perryville, MO. and married Simeon Sylvester Tucker (son of Joseph Tucker and Sarah Ann Miles);

and,

4-11.   Julia Cissell born ca. 1852.

Marker for Joseph Cissell (Senior) at the Mount Hope Cemetery, Perryville, MO in 1972:

Since Joseph died without a will, his estate was probated and so we know it was not insignificant for that time[42].   The heirs, as listed on the Administrator's Bond dated 1 Apr 1878, were: "Martena Tucker, Nerius Cissell's heirs, Vincent Cissell, Lewis Cissell, Pius Cissell's heirs, Joseph C Cissell's heirs, Mary A. Cissell (now Tucker). Mary J Cissell the widow of

---

[41] May be the same as Marietta Cissell who died 18 Sep 1872, age 4 in Perry County, MO.

[42] The 1st distribution of the Estate funds is not known, but the 2nd was for $6,400 and the 3rd for $3,440. Narcissus Cissell's share from these amounted to $182.84.

dec^d. all resident^s of Perry Co. Mo. Except Narcis Cissell child of Nerius Cissell who resides in Minnesota."

Narius (Nerius) Cissell, son of Joseph Cissell and Ann Miles, was born in Perry County, Mo. ca. 1819 and died there in Dec 1877. He married first Christina Hagan (daughter of James Aquilla Hagan and Mary Tucker), born 4 Jan 1820. Their children, all born in Perry County, MO. included:

1. **Nerius (Narcissus) Martin Cissell**. Born 18 Jan 1842. (Continued)

2. Mary Ann Cissell. Born 25 Jan 1844. Died 11 Apr 1909, Perry County, MO. Married Feriol Prevallet (son of Melchoir Prevallet and Jeanne ____) 31 Jul 1865 in Perryville, MO. Their children included: Albert M. (1 May 1866- ca. 1911); Mary Louise (22 Sep 1869-28 Feb 1907); Mary Genevieve (7 Jan 1872-17 Oct 1929); William Joseph (15 May 1874-   ); Mary Henrietta (Harriet) (30 Dec 1876-11 Apr 1912); and Mary Anna (1 Jul 1882-ca. 1929).

3. Lewis Clark Cissell. Born 11 Nov 1847. Died 14 Apr 1923. Married Anna Olivia Vessells (daughter of George Vessells and Alice Luttrell) 17 Apr 1871 in Perryville, MO. Children included: Emmett [43](1 Sep 1873-   ); Thomas Edwin (22 Feb 1875-19 Sep 1948); Charles Arthur (10 Oct 1877-5 May 1910); John Maurice (9 Dec 1879-4 Jan 1954); Joseph Elliot (7 Aug 1884-17 Jun 1950); Mary Olivia (2 Oct 1886-ca. 1956); Francis Lee (16 Jan 1889-13 Jan 1956); George (24 Jun 1893-by 1928); Daughter, died by 1928; and Nerius L. (Lonnie) (6 Feb 1895-Nov 1982).

4. Thomas Cissell. Born 4 Oct 1849. Died ca. 1870.

5. Julia Cissell. Born 17 Jan 1852. Died 3 Jul 1928 in Perryville, MO. Married Maurice(Moritz) Prevallet 6 Nov 1871 in Perryville, MO. Children, all born in Perry County, Mo., included: Mary (4 Sep 1872-   ); Ann Abella (16 May 1874-   ); Joseph (22 Feb 1876-   ); Thomas Elmore (11 Dec 1879-ca 1928); John Leonard (2 Jan 1884(5)-23 Feb 1950); Minnie (-ca. 1950); and Ernest M. (14 Jun 1890-6 Dec 1945)

6. Peter C. Cissell. Born 9 Sep 1855. Married America Burgee (daughter of Joab Waters Burgee and Elizabeth Burns) 13 Dec 1877

---

[43] Identified as "William" in the 1880 US census.

in Perryville, MO. Children included: Elizabeth Marie (1879-   );
Birdie; Julie; Clarence; Herman; Ella; Corine; and Grace.

7. Mary Caroline Cissell. Born 13 Dec 1862.

8. Robert Joseph Cissell. Born 23 Feb 1869.

9. Charles Joseph Cissell. Born 25 Aug 1872.

Christina Hagan died in Perry County, MO in May 1858 and is buried in the
Mount Hope Cemetery, Perryville, MO.

Marker for "Christenia Hagen" in 1972.

Narius Cissell, son of Joseph Cissell and Ann Miles, married secondly Julia
Brown, but no children are known. Narius is buried at the Mount Hope
Cemetery, Perryville, MO.

Narius (Nerius) obtained patents from the United States for land in Perry
County, Mo. in 1841 and 1856. A copy of one of the patents is shown on
the next page:

CERTIFICATE
No. *7398*

THE UNITED STATES OF AMERICA,

iq *37*

To all to whom these Presents shall come, Greeting:

WHEREAS *Nereus Cissell, of Perry County, Missouri,*

ha*s* deposited in the **GENERAL LAND OFFICE** of the United States, a Certificate of the **REGISTER OF THE LAND** OFFICE at *Jackson* whereby it appears that full payment has been made by the said *Nereus Cissell* according to the provisions of

the Act of Congress of the 24th of April, 1820, entitled "An Act making further provision for the sale of the Public Lands," for *the North West quarter of the South West quarter, and the South East quarter of the South West quarter of Section Twenty seven, in Township thirty five North, of Range ten East, in the District of Lands subject to sale at Jackson, Missouri, containing eighty acres,*

according to the official plat of the survey of the said Lands, returned to the General Land Office by the **SURVEYOR GENERAL**, which said tract has been purchased by the said *Nereus Cissell*

NOW KNOW YE, That the

United States of America, in consideration of the Premises, and in conformity with the several acts of Congress, in such case made and provided, *HAVE GIVEN AND GRANTED,* and by these presents *DO GIVE AND GRANT,* unto the said *Nereus Cissell*

and to *his* heirs, the said tract above described: **TO HAVE AND TO HOLD** the same, together with all the rights, privileges, immunities, and appurtenances of whatsoever nature, thereunto belonging, unto the said *Nereus Cissell*

and to *his* heirs and assigns forever.

In Testimony Whereof, I, *John Tyler,*

PRESIDENT OF THE UNITED STATES OF AMERICA, have caused these Letters to be made **PATENT,** and the SEAL of the **GENERAL LAND OFFICE** to be hereunto affixed.

GIVEN under my hand, at the **CITY OF WASHINGTON**, the *tenth* day of *December* in the Year of our Lord one thousand eight hundred and *forty one* and of the **INDEPENDENCE OF THE UNITED STATES** the Sixty *Sixth.*

[L.S.]

BY THE PRESIDENT: *John Tyler,*

By *R. Tyler* Sec'y.

J. Williamson RECORDER of the General Land Office.

1. Nerius (Narcissus) Martin Cissell, son of Narius Cissell and Christina Hagan, was born 18 Jan 1842 [44] in Perry County, Mo. and died 19 Mar 1906 in Ponoka, Alberta, Canada. Nerius is listed on the 1850 US Census as "Narcissus Cissel", age 8. {He may have had a tough childhood, if his family actually called him by that name. And, as indicated by Joseph Cissell's probate records, they very well may have.}

Nerius served in the Civil War as a private with Company "L", 5th Regiment, Missouri State Militia Calvary from 25 March 1862 to 24 March 1865.

After the conclusion of the Civil War, Nerius married Elizabeth E. (Alice Mary)[45] Bey, daughter of Felix Bey and Lucy Manch, on 12 June 1866 [46]. There was a sizable community of French immigrants in Perry County, and both of Alice's parents had been born in France. Alice had been born in Perry County on 8 Oct 1847.

---

[44] Latin records of the Church of the Assumption, Perryville, MO. record the baptism of Narrissum Martinum Cissell on the 2 of March 1842, son of Nerei Cissell and Christinia Hagen, born the 18 of January 1842.

[45] Elizabeth E. Bey seems to have adopted the name of "Alice Mary" and so that name is used for this book.

[46] Records of the Church of the Assumption, Perryville, MO.

4. Dodge County, Minnesota and Kingsbury County, South Dakota

After their marriage, Nerius Cissell and Alice Bey moved to Minnesota, near the town of Mantorville and about 14 miles west of Rochester. The 11 Jun 1870 US Census for Mantorville Township, Dodge County, MN lists N. Cissell, farmer age 29. Also listed is his wife Alice age 21; Leo age 2 and Manitta age 1, both children having been born in Minnesota. "Manitta" is taken to be their eldest daughter, Etta M. (Hettie) Cissell. The 16 Aug 1870 US Census also lists Narius with some of his siblings in St. Mary's Township, Perry County, MO, so he must have travelled back home that summer. If he did, it appears that his family did not accompany him. His occupation there was listed as Carpenter and Farmer.

The 1875 Minnesota State Census shows that the family had moved a few miles SW to Ashland Township, in Dodge County. Alice's brother, Frank Bey, had owned land in that Township as early as 1870 and had probably come there about 1865. Frank Bey may well have been the reason for Nerius and Alice moving to Minnesota in the first place. In 1894 Frank had the NW 1/4 of Section 33, the NW 1/4 of Section 34 and the adjacent N 1/2 of the SW 1/4 of Section 34. He also had the NW 1/4 of Section 3 in Hayfield Township, just S of his other land[47]. It could be that Nerius and Alice had been living temporarily in the Mantorville area until they could get land in Ashland Township near her brother. It is likely that Nerius was doing carpentry work as well as farming.

Nerius and Alice had at least 9 children, all born in Minnesota [48]:

  1. Leon Albert Cissell[49] (1868-1915). (Continued)
  2. Etta M. (Hettie, Mary, or Manitta) Cissell (1869 - ca. 1890). (Continued).
  3. Julia Cissell. Born 1871, died young before 1885.

---

[47] Frank and his family moved into the town of Mantorville about Jan 1893 and by 1895 Frank was identified as the County Treasurer.

[48] The 1900 SD census form indicates that Alice had had 5 children, but that only 4 (presumably Leon, Frank, Emma, and Bessie) were still alive. As Alice L. also seems to have still been alive at this time (and living next door), it is assumed that she was overlooked and that the 5th (and now deceased) child was likely Etta M.

[49] The origin of the name "Leon Albert" is not known, but it is noted that the town of "Albert Lea", MN is located about 30 miles SW of Dodge County and the couple may well have visited there.

4. Frank Cissell (1873- 1936). (Continued).
5. Alice L. Cissell (1 Jun 1875 - 29 Mar 1901). (Continued).
6. Willie Cissell. Born 21 Oct 1877 and died 19 Nov 1878.
7. Mary Cissell. Born 18 Jan (Feb?) 1880 and died 21 Jan 1881.
8. Emma R. Cissell (25 Aug 1883 - 30 Aug 1950). (Continued).
9. Carrie (Bessie) Cissell (1885 - 1947). (Continued).

The family was recorded on the 18 May 1885 Minnesota State census for Ashland, Dodge County. The family and their ages at this time were noted as:

N Cissell 43	Frank Cissell 12
Elle Cissell 36 [50]	Alice Cissell 9
Leio (or Leis) Cissell 17	Emma Cissell 2
Etta Cissell 16	Carrie Cissell 0

Sometime after Jun 1885 the family moved to the Dakota Territory. The exact date they moved is not known, but the birth dates of some of their grandchildren suggest it may have been by about 1889 or 1890. In addition, Nerius was listed on the June 1890 South Dakota Veterans census for Lake County and so the family had moved prior to that time. The Chicago and North Western railroad had come to the nearby town of Brookings by 1879 and one could assume that the family had been able to travel by train. South Dakota became a State on 2 Nov 1889, and so about the time that the Cissells arrived. The economic panic of 1893 did impact the area with effects lasting till 1897. In addition, drought conditions peaked around 1894 and so affected farming efforts at this time.

Although not evident in the family photos that survive, Nerius received some accidental injury during his Civil War service. Veterns with injuries were elligible for a Government pension. Prior to approving a pension, though, Congress had to determine that the injury was service related. To this end, a Report (No. 2948), was prepared for Nerius (Nirius) by the US House of Representatives in 1886. A copy is shown on the next two pages.

---

[50] The spelling for Nerius's wife here is of interest. The census enumerator (or assessor) was "Frank Bey", Alice's brother. It seems that he, as a family member, knew his sister more by her originally given name of "Elizabeth" instead of the "Alice" she seems to have adopted.

Report No. 2948:

NIRIUS CISSELL.

JUNE 22, 1886.—Committed to the Committee of the Whole House and ordered to be printed.

Mr. O'HARA, from the Committee on Invalid Pensions, submitted the following

REPORT:

[To accompany bill H. R. 9026.]

The Committee on Invalid Pensions, to whom was referred the bill (H. R. 9026) granting a pension to Nirius Cissell, have considered the same, and submit the following report:

Claimant enlisted March 25, 1862, private, Company L, Fifth Regiment, Missouri State Militia Cavalry; discharged March 24, 1865. Claim for pension filed January 5, 1881, and alleged that at Greenville, Mo., he was blown up in the explosion of a magazine tent—said explosion being accidental—by which his face was badly burned, causing weak eyes. Claim rejected on the ground that the alleged injury of eyes was not contracted in line of duty.

In this case there is no doubt as to soldier's prior soundness of sight, as to his receiving the injury complained of, nor of its continuance to date. The only question to be determined is was the soldier in the line of duty when he received the injury complained of?

Fred. Charvoux, first lieutenant of soldier's company, testifies:

On or about October 1, 1863, claimant became disabled while in line of duty by an explosion of a box of loose powder, while engaged in writing a letter, caused by another comrade coming in and snuffing the candle, throwing a spark into the box of loose powder, by which claimant's face, eyes, and head were badly burned, rendering him unfit for duty for a long time, and that he never was entirely cured. Affiant knows the foregoing facts by being called to the place immediately after the accident occurred.

Vincent Tucker and Thomas W. Robinson, comrades, testified in substance to the same state of facts.

The board of surgeons at Rochester, Minn., June 10, 1885, find as follows:

Upper and lower lids of both eyes inflamed and covered with granules, edges of lids excoriated and covered with thick whitish discharge. Can read text type only with difficulty and has to turn head to left, the effort causing a reddening of conjunctiva, and a profuse watery discharge ensues. The disease, chronic ophthalmia is of long standing. The disability is equivalent to loss of one eye.

The medical examiners that examined the case all pronounce the claim to be one of merit.

2   NIRIUS CISSELL.

We do not think that the accident was due to such carelessness of soldier as would warrant the rejection of the claim; notwithstanding the injury he served faithfully and without complaint the full period of three years for which he enlisted.

Your committee are of the opinion that soldier incurred his disability while in the line of duty and in the service of the United States, and is entitled to the relief asked for; therefore recommend that the bill do pass.

The report must have been acceptable as the Congress did officially grant Nerius (Nirius) a pension on 22 Feb 1887:

FORTY NINTH CONGRESS. Sess. II. Chs. 196–200. 1887.   **911**

CHAP. 196.—An act granting a pension to Nirius Cissell.   Feb. 22, 1887.

Be it enacted by the Senate and House of Representatives of the United States of America in Congress assembled, That the Secretary of the Interior be, and he is hereby, authorized and directed to place on the pension-roll, subject to the provisions and limitations of the pension laws, the name of Nirius Cissell, late of Company L, Fifth Regiment Missouri Cavalry.

Approved, February 22, 1887.

Nirius Cissell. Pension.

The 1900 census shows that the family of Nerius, Alice M., Emma R., and Bessie M. were living in the town of Oldham, Spring Lake Township, Kingsbury County, SD. Nerius's grandson, Frank D. Davis, was also living with them; his birth date was noted as being Mar 1890. Alice L. and her husband Richard J. Mueller were living next door. Leon and his family were also living nearby in town. Frank and his family lived slightly outside of town. They could have formed a small family construction company in addition to what farming they were doing, as Nerius and Leon were carpenters and Frank was a mason. Leon is known to have built many homes in Oldham[51].

---

[51] According to George Houk as quoted in a letter to Claud Cissell from Charles Madill of Ramona, SD, dated 15 Dec 1941, in family records.

An early photo shows the family near Madison SD[52]:

In the front row are Nerius Cissell, Bessie Cissell and Alice Bey. In the back row are Frank Cissell, Alice Cissell and Leon Cissell. The girl in the center is Emma Cissell. The object being displayed by Alice Bey is difficult to discern[53].

---

[52] Estimates of the ages of the children in the photo by Ashley Taleck suggest that the photo was likely taken in 1889 or possibly very early in 1890. The absence of Etta also supports this.

[53] It is likely a photo of Etta who was ill or had recently died.

A photo of the family was taken in the mid- to late- 1890's:

In the back row from left to right are Clara Thorsness, Leon Cissell, Cora Wing, Frank Cissell, Alice L. Cissell, and Richard Mueller. In the front row from left to right are Emma Cissell, Nerius Cissell[54], Alice Bey Cissell, and Bessie Cissell.

---

[54] Note: Nerius is wearing his Civil War, Grand Army of the Republic Badge. The badge was of bronze, made from cannons captured in battle during the Civil War, and is in a form of a five-pointed star. Alice seems to have been wearing a related item.

5. Ponoka, Alberta

In the late 1890s, Dakota had been suffering with bad weather, drought, and insect problems. After a couple of crop failures and seeing wheat drifting across the roads in wind storms, some decided they had lived on the prairie long enough. At the same time Canada had opened land for immigrants in the Northwest Territories, from which Alberta was later carved. A group of Dakota neighbors considered moving there seeking better farmland. Two of them, David Wing (father of Frank Cissell's wife, Cora) and Ebenezer Olmstead, went to investigate and returned with good reports. Land next to the Canadian Pacific Railroad (CPR) line could be purchased from CPR for about $200 per quarter section (160 acres). Land further away could be purchased from the Government for $10 with title given in three years if required improvements were made each year[55]. The group chose the less expensive option for land. The land they selected was about 15 miles from Ponoka on the trail[56] that lead west from the town. They stood on that trail at a small knoll, SE of the present Dakota Church and cemetery, and selected six or seven homesteads, all joining right around the present church; in fact the church and community center are currently on two of them[57]. Ponoka, itself, had originally been created as a stop or station for the CPR.

The first group from Dakota to move north included:

1. David and Hattie Wing
2. Lemuel and Ella Wing, child Rose; and Ella's children, Dan, Carl, Harvey, Mark and Scott Courser.
3. Corliss and Hattie (Royce) Wing and children, Genevieve and Vina
4. Rodney Royce and son George
5. Frederick and Clarissa (Wing) Bresee
6. Edgar and Clara (Hoar) Bresee
7. Frank and Cora (Wing) Cissell and children, Florence and George. They arrived in Ponoka about Nov 1900.
8. Ebenezer and Alice Olmstead and children, Abbie and Byron; and

---

[55] Upon taking up the homestead, the individual was required to clear at least 10 acres of land, undertake some cultivation, have built a habitable dwelling and some farm buildings, and live on the land for six months a year for three years. Once these requirements were met, the individual would submit an application for title (letters patent) to the land.

[56] The direct straight-line distance was about 10 miles, but the trail did not go in a straight line.

[57] Per Merl Cissell.

Ben and Olive (Ebenezer's children by his first wife)
9. Dan Kilroy and wife
10. Mrs. Mary E. Hall and children.

The Cissell family stayed together as it had done in the past; Nerius and Alice immigrating in 1902 and Leon following in 1905. Frank's land was the Northwest quarter of Section 22, Township 43, Range 27, West of the 4th Meridian.

Although perhaps not noticed by most urban residents, much of the United States (and Alberta) has been surveyed and laid out with a rectangular coordinate system. A series of "base lines" running east/west and "principle meridians" running north/south have been established and form the basis for the system. "Townships", 6 miles on a side, are then laid out in rows north and south of the base lines and east and west of the prime meridians.

Township designations indicate the location north or south of the baseline, and range designations indicate the location east or west of the Principal Meridian. For example Frank's land was in the 43rd row of townships north of the Canadian/US Border and in the 27th column of townships west of the 4th principle meridian (defined as longitude 102 degrees, just west of the Manitoba Saskatchewan border).

Each Township is then subdivided into 36 "Sections" of 1 mile on a side. Each of these 36 Sections is numbered with defined pattern. In Canada the numbering starts in the lower right (SE) corner of the Township. In the United States, the numbering starts in the upper right (NE) corner of the Township.

31	32	33	34	35	36
30	29	28	27	26	25
19	20	21	22	23	24
18	17	16	15	14	13
7	8	9	10	11	12
6	5	4	3	2	1

6	5	4	3	2	1
7	8	9	10	11	12
18	17	16	15	14	13
19	20	21	22	23	24
30	29	28	27	26	25
31	32	33	34	35	36

Frank's land in Section 22, then, was near the center of the township.

Each of the 1-mile square sections can be, and frequently are, further subdivided into quarters, such as the "NW 1/4 of Section 22". As a measure of land, a quarter section is 160 acres and a "quarter-quarter section" is 40 acres. Frank's land then was the entire NW quarter of section 22 and so consisted of 160 acres.

Nerius had made a homesteading claim for the Southwest 1/4 of Section 16, Township 43, Range 27 on 22 Feb 1901. So Nerius's land would have been a bit SW of Frank's. On that same day, Leon (as Leo A. Cissell) had claimed the land just to the East of Nerius's (the Southeast 1/4 of Section 16, Township 43, Range 27).

Nerius could not immediately go to his land because of problems in selling his property in Oldham. So he needed an extension for the homestead application. In a letter to the Canadian Department of the Interior in Aug 1901 he wrote,"...My reason for an extension is (I) can't sell my property here before Fall to go there. Will go as soon as I can..."

He finally did reach the property on 18 Jan 1902. The subsequent arrival of Alice Bey and two of her daughters (Bessie and Emma) to Ponoka was reported on page 6 of the Edmonton Bulletin newspaper on 10 Feb 1902:

> "Ponoka .... Mrs. Nerius Cissell and daughters Miss Bessie, and Mrs. Amo Wall[58], arrived from Oldham, S.D., Friday, to join her husband who had proceeded. Mr. Wall arrived with the car yesterday."

Nerius and Alice hosted a Christmas dance at their home on Friday 19 Dec 1902 for about 80 people. Emil Wold and Bessie Cissell provided the music for the event.

Because of the large influx of immigrants from Dakota, the area became known as the Dakota District.

The Dakota Cemetery Association was formed at a meeting in the Dakota District on 9 May 1903. The cemetery was established as a community graveyard, open to anyone regardless of religious affiliation or ability to pay. The cemetery and one grave was moved from a site one mile south to its present location[59] before 1904; the land having been donated by

---

[58] The newspaper spelling of "Emil Wold's" name seems to have been done somewhat phonetically.

[59] [52.72883, -113.846506].

Ebenezer Rockwell Olmstead and David Wing. David was one of the first of the Dakota settlers to be buried there and was buried as near the center of the cemetery as possible. The original fee for a plot was $2.00, with community members always digging the graves free of charge.

The Dakota Cemetery as it appeared in 1972.

In the early days, Ebenezer Olmstead and Cora Cissell were called on to do the undertaking, while Frank and Leon Cissell made many of the caskets. Bob Tiltgen, with his black horse team and democrat wagon, transported many to their last resting place.

In this early period, the farmers would use a horse-powered thresher. It worked up one side of the Battle River and down the other, usually finishing on Christmas Day. Swamp fever killed many of the settler's horses. Oxen yokes were made from double or branched trees.

For firewood, green trees were cut down and hauled on a bobsleigh to an open yard. Then the neighbors all got together and spent the day sawing the pile of wood. There was enough to last for a year, and then the splitting took place.[60]

---

[60] Per Emma Cissell Olmstead.

Sawing lumber at Herrick's farm. Rear (L to R): Uknown, Marcus Grandall, Frank Cissell, Unknown, Orion Herrick (on Wheel). Front (L to R): Claud "Ole" Cissell with a pipe wrench, Unknown, Friglam, Leon Cissell. Boys: Lyle and Alvin Herrick.

Nerius died 19 Mar 1906 and, like the other Dakota District settlers, was buried in the Dakota Cemetery[61].

---

[61] Block 16. [52.732989, -113.847711].

The marker for Nerius Cissell[62]

The settlement of Nerius's estate is of interest, mainly because of the time it took to be completed.

The Supreme Court of the North West Territories made his wife, Alice Mary Cissell, administrator of his estate on 23 Jan 1907. Alice died on 14 Jul 1924 without having fully administered the Estate. So on 11 Dec 1928 the District Court of Northern Alberta assigned administration of the Estate to Nerius's son, Frank Cissell. Frank Cissell died 15 May 1936 leaving the estate of his father still un-administered. So the District Court

---

[62] The marker for Nerius was provided by the U.S. Government because of his Civil War service. The inscription refers to Company L, 5th (Missouri) Regiment, Missouri State Militia Calvary. During the war, Company L had been commanded by Captain P. Hagan.

of Northern Alberta then assigned administration of the Estate to Frank's son, Walter Merl Cissell, on 12 Jan 1937. Walter completed his actions by 4 Jul 1945. Final Court decisions were then rendered on 30 Aug 1945; 39 years after Nerius's death.

After allowing for Court directed payments, approximately $341.68 remained to be distributed in August 1945. Court reported or directed payments up to that time had been:

$393.85 Administrator (Walter)
$175.03 Cora E. Cissell, Daughter-in-law (Frank's wife & Walter's mother)
$171.53 Lawyer
$100.00 Emma, Daughter
$100.00 Bessie, Daughter
$60.00   Frank Davis (estate of)
$14.26   Claude Cissell, Grandson
$14.26   Albert Cissell, Grandson
$14.26   Vera (Pat), Granddaughter
$14.26   Clarence Beacock, Grandson
$14.26   Harry Cissell, Grandson
$8.56   William (Bill) Cissell, Grandson
$5.70   Ernest Cissell, Grandson

People travelling from Homeglen and elsewhere to Ponoka by horse team or oxen would often stop at Alice Cissell's house to rest. Nerius had erected the grey tin-sided house among the spruce trees in Feb 1902.

Alice and Nerius's home no longer stands, but this is how it looked in 1972:

On 12 Jul 1912, Alice married a neighbor, Fredrick Ortman, (born about Jun 1850 in Germany and son of George Ortman and Minna Vede). But she soon separated from him.

Alice's daughter-in-law, Clara Thorsness died in 1913. Alice assumed responsibility for helping to raise most of Clara and Leon's children as well as Alice's grandson, Frank Davis, who she still had responsibility for. Leon died in July 1915 leaving the children fully in her care. But she had experienced even worse problems with her estranged husband earlier that year.

From The Western Globe newspaper (of Lacombe, Alberta, Canada), March 31, 1915, Page 3:

"...Fred Ortman, aged 67, living thirteen miles west of Ponoka, made an attempt to murder his wife on Monday (29 March), and then committed suicide.

Mr. and Mrs. Ortman have been living apart for some time, Mrs. Ortman with her grandchildren, and her husband with other relatives. On Monday the husband laid in wait in the barn for Mrs. Ortman, who he knew would be out to milk the cows. On her appearance, without any warning, he fired two revolver shots at her, one going through her right arm and the other grazing her breast and going into her left arm. She fell to the ground and Ortman, thinking he had killed her, turned the revolver against himself and fired a shot into his breast, dying instantly.

The police were notified immediately, and Corp. Wells went up from here to look into the case. As the facts were self-evident, no inquest was held on Ortman. Mrs. Ortman will recover, although she is suffering greatly fro(m) shock and being an old lady, over 60 years, complications may ensue."

And similarly, but with slightly wrong dates, from the Edmonton Bulletin of April 1, 1915, page 2:

"....Ponoka, March 31 - A tragedy occurred Tuesday morning at Bismark, fourteen miles west of Ponoka, when Fred Ortman attempted to kill his wife and then committed suicide. The couple had been living apart for about a year. Deceased entered the barn where Mrs. Ortman had gone to milk and fired two shots both lodging in her arms. He then turned the revolver on himself putting a bullet through his chest. Death was instantaneous. Mr. Ortman was born in Germany and had served a term in the navy. He came to Alberta several years ago and was a highly respected citizen."

By 1920, Alice, the Leon Cissell family members under her care, and her daughter Bessie's family, had all returned to the United States. Her granddaughter, Vera, had returned to the States in 1916. Most of the family settled in Yakima, Washington.

One of Alice's sons, Frank, did not return to the United States. He and his family continued to farm near Ponoka. Frank Cissell, Cora Wing, and their family are discussed in the next Chapter and so close the Ponoka part of the family history.

6. Frank Cissell

Frank Cissell, son of Nerius Cissell and Alice Mary Bey, was born 26 Sep 1873 in Ashland Township, Dodge County, MN. His name was most likely taken from that of his mother's brother, Frank Bey. He married Cora Emalyne Wing on 1 July 1894 in Madison, Lake County, SD.

Cora had been born on 27 Mar 1876 in Sutton, Brome County, Quebec, Canada. Her parents were David Wing and Julia Elvina Hadlock. The Wings and other farming families[63] had traveled from Sutton to Kansas in 1877 and settled briefly in Sumner Township, KS.

The Wing's trip from Quebec to Kansas had been made by wagon train. One of their experiences was that they came to the Missouri river and had to wait four days for it to freeze over. As later related by their grandson, Merl Cissell:

> "Now they just had mules and a few shoes, so they shod a few mules and as they went across on the ice, the corks[64] cut through the ice. The ones they didn't have shoes for, one man got on each side with a short cercingle[65] to keep it from falling and possibly breaking through. They took the wagon across on ropes so as not to have too much weight at once."

The area in Kansas did not suit them and by 1881 they had moved to Lake County, SD. Cora's mother, Julia, died there on 10 Apr 1892, age 38 Years, 8 months. After her mother's death and before David Wing remarried[66], Cora lived with a neighbor, Rodney Royce. His wife, Amanda Ives Royce, had recently died.

Frank and Cora lived on a farm in Kingsbury County, outside of Oldham in Spring Lake Township. In addition to farming, Frank also worked as a mason. Their children born in SD included:

---

[63] The Wings were Seventh-day Adventists.

[64] Metal pegs that are screwed into the animal's metal shoe that act like cleats and so provide traction for the animal walking on ice.

[65] Or surcingle; a leather strap around the animal's upper chest.

[66] David returned to his home in Quebec and married Anna Mullen on June 15, 1893, in Richford, VT, just across the border from Sutton.

1. Florence M. Cissell, born Mar 1895. (Continued.)
2. George Wing Cissell, born Sep 1896. (Continued.)

The weather in South Dakota could become a little rough on occasion as was reported by a contemporary newspaper[67]:

WRECKED BY HURRICANE.

Lake County Suffered From Wind and Rain.

Madison, S. D., Special, June 8.—A hurricane passed over this county Saturday evening. The northwestern part was most severely struck. Reports come in to-day of twenty or more barns and several houses that were wrecked. Mrs. Frank Cissel and girl were in a house which was totally destroyed. The former had her collar bone broken and the later her fac cut. Many wind mills were wrecked. Three inches of water fell during the day, accompanied by a heavy electrical storm. Five residences in Madison were struck by lightning. No fatalities.

The "Mrs. Frank Cissel" was Cora Wing Cissell and the "girl" was her daughter, Florence[68]. The storm was clearly a tornado.

As indicated earlier, Frank and his family moved to Ponoka about Nov 1900. There they had five more children:

3. Raymond C. Cissell, Born 1902. (Contined)
4. Lodema Thelma Cissell, born 5 Sep 1905. (Continued.)
5. Emma Lottie Cissell, born 17 Feb 1910. (Continued.)
6. Walter Merl Cissell, born 13 Aug 1914. (Continued.)
7. Unnamed infant, born and died 1916.

After arriving in Ponoka, Frank and Cora occupied a house that had been built in 1899 by Ebenezer Olmstead and Corliss Wing. They moved out to their homestead (NW 22) in the spring of 1901.

---

[67] The Saint Paul (Minnesota) Globe for Tuesday June 9 1896, page 3.
[68] Judy Cissell Miller Jones noted that Florence Cissell McClaflin's grandchildren remembered her always wearing her hair down over part of her forehead to hide the scar she had gotten from this storm.

Medical care was hard to get so Cora acted as nurse and mid-wife, ultimately helping the delivery of over 200 babies. Cora would also care for a sick person in her own home when needed. Frank helped many people with his blacksmith shop. He also built and plastered many homes in the area.

Cora, along with George Hoar, were the first Trustees of the Dakota Cemetery and she held this position until her death[69]. The Cissell home was host to many community get-togethers.

Cora Wing, Lodema, and Frank Cissell about 1909

The family took their holidays in August at blueberry time. They took a tent, a supply of food and plenty of boxes for blueberries. They had two horse drawn vehicles and went up to the south of Battle Lake. They usually camped by a spring, so had plenty of water and a cool place to keep their food and cream. Fresh blueberries and cream always helped make a good meal. They always got all the berries they could use. The berries also provided for pies to serve at social gatherings at their home[70].

[69] In fact, the names of the trustees were not officially updated until 2006, when an application was made for a grant to improve the cemetery.
[70] Remembrance provided by Emma Cissell Olmstead.

One story later related by Emma Cissell Olmstead, told of returning home with her brother Merl one morning after having spent the night at Florence and Lynn McClaflin's house. They found Cora standing by a cupboard with her face all black and blue, a big gash over her eye and one on her cheek; the eye was nearly swollen shut. Frank was sitting at the table reading a paper with a smug look on his face. The children asked what had happened, and Cora replied, "Ask him, he did it." Frank's response was, "It was harder on me than her." It turned out that they had been separating the milk; Frank had the separating machine speed nearly up when he decided the cream spout needed to be moved a bit. In so doing the separator bowl caught the spout and sent them flying at great speed. Cora had just poured two pails of milk into the tank of the machine and was standing nearby. The tank was knocked off, spilling all the milk and the spout hit Cora in the face. Frank said, "All she did was sit by the basin and hold wet clothes on her face, while I had to mop up those two pails of milk off the stand and the separator room floor."

Emma provided another story of this time:

> "I remember when we had to bail water out of a 20 ft. well with a tin pail. If you could flip the pail just right you could get a pail full of water, but if not flipped right you would not get a pail full and that pail would float. It took a long time to fill that water trough for the cows or the horses, when the men came in from the field."

Frank died 15 May 1936. Cora died 3 Mar 1940. Both are buried in the Dakota Cemetery. Their children remained in Canada:

1. Florence May Cissell, daughter of Frank Cissell and Cora Wing, was born 28 Mar 1895 in Madison County, SD. She married Lynn Horatio McClaflin on 7 Oct 1913 at Lacombe, Alberta. Lynn was born 16 Jan 1893 and died in Ponoka, Alberta 19 Sep 1953. Florence died 10 Jan 1966 in Ponoka, Alberta. Both are buried in the Dakota Cemetery. Florence and Lynn had 9 children, all born in Ponoka:

1-1. Wilfred McClafin, born Jul 1914 and died that same month.

1-2. Wilton Lawerence McClafin, born 1 Jun 1915, married Irene Lydia Webster 25 Sep 1949 in Ponoka. Irene, the daughter of Findley Webster and Lydia Merrell, was born 25 Dec 1930. They had 7 children, all born in Ponoka:

1-2-1. Wade L. McClaflin, born 29 Jul 1952, married Candice Scovoranski in 1973; this marriage ended in divorce. Wade married secondly Kristiene Sagert on 15 Aug 1978. Wade had three children.

> 1-2-1-1. Cameron Lawrence Rice[71], born 1 Mar 1974. He married Teresa Mason (born 19 Sep 1973) on 4 Oct 1997. This marriage ended in divorce, but they had three children.
>
>> 1-2-1-1-1. Cooper Rice, born 18 Aug 2000.
>>
>> 1-2-1-1-2. Jared Rice, born 31 Oct 2001.
>>
>> 1-2-1-1-3. Parker Rice, born 16 Jan 2004.
>
> 1-2-1-2. Daniel Lawrence McClaflin, born 11 Mar 1981. Married Tricia Thomson (born 1 Jun 1981) on 22 May 2004. They had a daughter:
>
>> 1-2-1-2-1. Lillya Grace McClaflin, born 14 Jul 2011.
>
> 1-2-1-3 Nathan William McClaflin, born 26 Mar 1985.

1-2-2. Gerald Lynn McClaflin, born 19 Nov 1954. Married Susan Angela Kasur (born 15 Jul 1960) on 26 Aug 1989.

1-2-3. Clayton Del McClaflin, born 16 May 1956. Married Diane Issac (born 31 Mar 1956) on 18 Oct 1975. They had two children:

> 1-2-3-1. Brian McClaflin, born 25 Apr 1984. Married Amanda ___ (born 21 Sep 1984) on 27 Jun 2011.
>
> 1-2-3-1. Charisse Audrey McClaflin, born 4 Feb 1986 at Redwater, AB.

---

[71] Cameron McClaflin took his mother's second marriage name of "Rice"

1-2-4. Miles Lee McClaflin, born 17 Dec 1960. Married Kimberly Jane Onesto (born 22 Jan 1967) on 14 Feb 1987. They had two children:

1-2-4-1. Colton McClaflin, born 16 Apr 1991.

1-2-4-2. Destyn McClaflin, born 14 Jan 1994.

1-2-5. Roxanne Lydia McClaflin, born 1 Apr 1960. Married Leon Algadzis on 2 Sep 1989. This marriage ended in divorce, but they had two children.

1-2-5-1. Elanta Algadzis , born 11 Feb 1995.

1-2-5-2. Caleb Algadzis , born 24 Jul 1997.

1-2-6. Lorne Ward McClaflin, born 23 Apr 1967. Married Shirley Sommer (born 2 Feb 1967) on 8 Oct 1988. They had five children.

1-2-6-1. Zachary McClaflin, born 26 Feb 1990.

1-2-6-2. Brandi Lynn McClaflin, born 25 Apr 1991.

1-2-6-3. Kirk Gordon McClaflin, born 27 Nov 1992, died 22 May 1993.

1-2-6-4. Katelyn McClaflin, born 21 Oct 1995.

1-2-6-5. Lucas McClaflin, born 21 Oct 1995 and died that same day.

1-2-7. Twilla Joy McClaflin, born 11 Aug 1969. Had two children:

1-2-7-1. Tristan McClaflin, born 18 Feb 1987.

1-2-7-2. Brenten McClaflin, born 15 Nov 1989.

1-3. Pearl Opal Geraldine McClaflin, born 16 Jul 1916. Married first Anthony Kessler on 21 Jul 1937. Anthony was born 29 Dec 1914 in Granlea, Alberta and was the son of John Kessler and Magdalenna Wentz. They had seven children. The Wood's

Homes Orphanage in Calgary raised most of the children, after Anthony's death:

1-3-1.   Noreen Kessler, born 3 Sep 1938 in Ponoka, married Gerald Ryall (born 4 Jun 1940). They had four children.

    1-3-1-1. Jerry Ryall, born 10 May 1958.

    1-3-1-2. Janet Ryall, born 22 Nov 1959.

    1-3-1-3. Larry Ryall, born 8 Jan 1964.

    1-3-1-4. Terry Ryall, born 15 Feb 1965.

1-3-2.   Garry Kessler, born 30 Dec 1939 in Ponoka married Margaret Anne Hoszouski (born 30 May 1946) on 16 May 1964.   Garry died in 1996 and Margaret in 2002. They had a daughter:

    1-3-2-1. Julie Kessler, born 8 May 1972.

1-3-3.   Esther Kessler, born 20 Aug 1941 in Calgary, Alberta. Married Fred Van Abs (born 25 Mar 1932). They had two children.

    1-3-3-1. Kenny Van Abs, born 21 Sep 1965. Married Paige Thompson in Nov 1983, but the marriage ended in divorce.

    1-3-3-2. Lawrence Van Abs, born 21 Sep 1965.

1-3-4. August Kessler, born 12 Aug 1942 in Calgary. Married Lil Montika. They had two children.

    1-3-4-1. Tammy Kessler, born 4 Jul 1976.

    1-3-4-2. Travis Kessler, born 7 Nov 1981.

1-3-5. Orville Duane Kessler, born 16 Jul 1943 in Calgary. Married Sharon Fraser (born 9 Jul 1945) on 11 Dec 1964. They had two children.

1-3-5-1.   Teresa Fay Kessler, born 27 Sep 1966. Married first Scott Bloomfield on 23 Jul 1988. This marriage ended in divorce on 8 Aug 1995. Teresa married secondly, Duane Green (born 21 Mar 1960) on 8 Jul 2000. Teresa and Scott's children include:

> 1-3-5-1-1.   Lee Russell Bloomfield, born 16 Oct 1986.

> 1-3-5-1-2.   Dean Bloomfield, born 25 Jun 1989.

> 1-3-5-1-3.   Brett Bloomfield, born 11 Jul 1992.

1-3-5-2.   Nancy May Kessler, born 27 May 1969. Married Mike Mochid (born 27 Dec 1965) on 24 Aug 1990. The marriage ended in divorce. There were four children associated with this family:

> 1-3-5-2-1.   Nicole Mochid, born 27 Apr 1985 was a stepdaughter to Nancy.

> 1-3-5-2-2.   Jeff Michael Mochid, born 28 Oct 1989.

> 1-3-5-2-3.   Steven Edward Mochid, born 29 May 1991.

> 1-3-5-2-4.   Miranda May Mochid, born 24 Nov 1994.

1-3-6.   Faye Lottie Kessler, born 11 Dec 1944 in Calgary. Died 29 Jul 1963.

1-3-7.   Juanita Betty Kessler, born 16 Jun 1946 in Calgary. She was officially adopted by Milton and Emma Olmstead. She married Donald Robert Allen on 27 Jun 1964. Donald had been born 1 Oct 1939 and was the son of Harold Allen and Goldie Mabbatt. Their children included:

> 1-3-7-1.   Deborah Juanita Allen, born 6 Jan 1966. She married Leon Wiancko on 17 Oct 1992. Leon was born 11 Oct 1961. Their children included:

1-3-7-1-1.   Ashley Juanita Wiancko, born 18 Feb 1994.

1-3-7-1-2.   Alyssa Dawn Wiancko, born 4 May 1999.

1-3-7-1-3.   Leanne Deborah Wiancko, born 4 May 1999.

1-3-7-2. Dwayne Donald Allen, born 27 May 1968 married Elaine Sarah Epp. Elaine was born 3 Jun 1975. Their family included:

1-3-7-2-1. Leigh Gordon Lyons, a stepchild to Dwayne, born 17 Jul 1994.
1-3-7-2-2. Monica Elaine Allen, born 10 Jan 2004.
1-3-7-2-3. Jonathan Dwayne Allen, born 14 Jan 2006.

Anthony died about 20 Jun 1946 in Calgary. Pearl Opal Kesler married secondly William Nagel (born 24 Aug 1910) 10 Apr 1971. Pearl Opal died in 1984.

1-4. Leaolla Bell McClaflin, born 20 Apr 1920, married Oswald Jensen 24 Mar 1939. Oswald was born 15 Feb 1903 in Denmark. Oswald died 9 April 1972 in Bashaw, Alberta. Leaolla died 17 Mar 1959 in Ponoka. Both are buried in Dakota Cemetery. They had three children all born in Ponoka:

1-4-1. Carl Lawrence Jensen, born 16 Feb 1945 and married Carol Newton 15 Aug 1964 in Ponoka. Carol was born 20 Feb 1945 and was the daughter of Guy Newton and Faye Donegby. Their family included:

1-4-1-1.   Randy Jensen, born 5 Apr 1967 in Edmonton was adopted by Carl and Carol. Married first Maureen Hall on 11 Jul 1998. This marriage ended with divorce. Randy married secondly, Trish McPhee (born 3 Oct 1966) on 26 Sep 2004. Trish's children included Bryce McPhee born 20 Oct 1994 and Darby McPhee, born 18 Oct 1996.

1-4-1-2.   Coleen Jensen, born 12 Feb 1968 in Ponoka. Married Todd Gadd (born 1 Jan 1968) on 13 Jun 1987. They had two daughters.

> 1-4-1-2-1. Carlynn Brandi Gadd, born 18 Jan 1991 in Red Deer, AB. Married Joshua Sookial 14 Jun 2014.

> 1-4-1-2-2. Shayla Dusty Gadd, born 13 May 1993.

1-4-1-3.   Jacqualine Jensen, born 12 Nov 1969 in Calgary was adopted by Carl and Carol. She married Darren Paulovich (born 4 Jul 1967) on 26 Aug 1995. Children included Braasen Carl John Paulovich, born 9 Jan 2002 in Lac La Biche, AB.

1-4-1-4.   Carmen Jensen, born 13 Oct 1971 in Ponoka. Married Gary Tebb (Born 16 May 1969) on 10 Aug 1991. Children included.

> 1-4-1-4-1. Niklas Carsen Tebb, born 29 Aug 2002.

> 1-4-1-4-2. Nathan Gary Tebb, born 28 Jan 2005.

1-4-1-5. Janelle Jensen, born 5 Jun 1979. Married Clayton Weigum (born 2 Apr 1979) on 15 Aug 1998. Children included.

> 1-4-1-5-1. Charlese Sylvia Weigum, born 3 Feb 2005 in Sundre, AB.

> 1-4-1-5-2. Carl Jayce Clayton Weigum, born 11 Jun 2008, Sunre, AB.

> 1-4-1-5-3. Bentley Marcus Weigum, born 12 Sep 2011, Olds, AB.

1-4-2. Linda May Jensen, born 24 Jan 1946 in Ponoka and married William Turner on 9 Jun 1967 in Ponoka.

William was born 10 Apr 1942 and was the son of Calvin Turner. Their children included:

> 1-4-2-1. Chris William Turner, born 21 Jan 1970 in Ponoka. Married Kathy Lynn Howard (born 8 Aug 1973) on 25 Jul 1998.

> 1-4-2-2. Quintin Lee Turner, born 11 Mar 1971 in Ponoka. Married Lori Fraser (born 12 Jun 1970) on 11 Jun 1994. Children included:

> > 1-4-2-2-1. Calvin Gerald Turner, born 17 Jan 1997.

> > 1-4-2-2-2. Kimberly Leanne Turner, born 29 Dec 1998.

> 1-4-2-3. Kathryn Jean Turner, born 13 Mar 1972 in Ponoka. Married Gary Geigle (born 13 Oct 1946) on 12 Jun 2012.

1-4-3. Janet Marie Jensen, born 1 Jul 1958 in Ponoka. Married Michael Ernest Barnes (born 1 Aug 1954) on 1 Sep 1979. They had one son:

> 1-4-3-1. Mathew Zacariah Barnes, born 26 Jan 1981. He married Roxanne Ferren on 24 Nov 2001, but the marriage ended in divorce.

1-5. Audrey Violet McClaflin, born 6 Feb 1922, married Chad Warnock (born 10 Jun 1922) on 1 Aug 1949. Audrey died 26 Mar 1990 and Chad on 3 Jun 1990.

1-6. Myrtle May McClaflin, born 10 May 1924, married William F. Hill (born 10 Jun 1922, Broadview, SK.) in 1948. Mrytle died 25 Feb 1982 and William on 11 Nov 2002. They had three children:

> 1-6-1. Deanna Muirene _____, born 22 Sep 1943 in Ponoka. William Hill raised Deanna as his own daughter. She married Floyd Norman McLeod (born 30 Sep 1943 in NB) on 24 May 1964. Deanna died 22 Dec 2008. They had one son:

1-6-1-1. Floyd Norman Martin McLeod, born 29 Aug 1965. Married _____, but the marriage ended in divorce. He married several more times. Children included:

> 1-6-1-1-1. Floyd William Connar McLeod, born 4 Jul 1989.

> 1-6-1-1-2. Callum McLeod, born 9 Oct 1995.

1-6-2. Lana Belle Hill, born 29 Jan 1949 in Calgary. Married first Dan Mowbray, but the marriage ended in divorce. Married secondly, Bruce Wilson and this marriage also ended in divorce. Married thirdly, Don Pascoe on 21 Jun 1986. In addition to a stepdaughter, Elizabeth Pascoe, Lana's children included:

> 1-6-2-1. John William Mowbray, born 8 Jun 1966. John did marry and had a daughter:

> > 1-6-2-1-1. Alicia Mowbray.

> 1-6-2-2. Steven Wilson, born 21 Aug 1969, Fredericton, NB.

> 1-6-2-3. Kory Michael Wilson, born 7 Jul 1975, Fredericton, NB.

> 1-6-2-4. Dawn Marie Wilson, born 30 Nov 1977 in NB.

1-6-3. Florence Hill, born 27 Mar 1953 in Calgary. Children included:

> 1-6-3-1. Kelly Jean Tooke, born 8 Aug 1968.

> 1-6-3-2. Jody Mae Fraser, born 19 Feb 1976. Jody had a daughter:

> > 1-6-3-2-1. Jenna.

1-7. Walter Gordon McClaflin, born 7 Feb 1927, married Doreen Joy Lux (born 24 Jun 1927, the daughter of Ray Lux and Etta Perry 3 Sep 1948 in Ponoka. They had two children:

1-7-1. Dwain Merl McClaflin, born 15 Jul 1951. Died 12 Apr 2007.

1-7-2. Diane Lynn McClaflin, born 26 Jan 1955. Married John Forbes Brown (born 22 Jan 1954) on 30 Jul 1977. Children included:

> 1-7-2-1. Cassandra Doreen Brown, born 3 Aug 1982.

> 1-7-2-2. Elissa Alexandra Brown, born 18 Jul 1984.

> 1-7-2-4. Patrick John Walker Brown, born 17 Mar 1988.

1-8. Thelma Lottie McClaflin, born 29 Oct 1929, married Kenneth Riddiough on 26 Jun 1949. Thelma died 12 Dec 1970 in Calgary and is buried there in Mountain View Memorial Cemetery[72]. They had two children born in Ponoka:

1-8-1. Keith Hartley Riddiough, born 24 Jun 1954. Married Barb Bannister (born 12 Dec 1957) on 20 Jun 1975. Barb died in Jun 2012. Children included:

> 1-8-1-1. Shane Hartley Riddiough, born 5 May 1980. Shane had a daughter:

>> 1-8-1-1-1. Kaida Riddiough, born Dec 2005.

> 1-8-1-2. Kurt Andrew Riddiough, born 2 Jul 1983.

1-8-2. Kevin George Riddiough, born 15 Jun 1955. Married Claire Louise Rode (born 15 Aug 1957) on 30 Aug 1975. Children included:

> 1-8-2-1. Marcy Riddiough, born 30 Mar 1979. Married Landon Nikirk (born 20 Aug 1976) on 13 May 2000. Children included:

>> 1-8-2-1-1. Brett Landon Riddiough, born 3 Oct 2001.

---

[72] Kenneth married secondly, Jean Boyce on 24 Feb 1973.

1-8-2-1-2.   Brody Dylan Riddiough, born 17 Apr 2003.

1-8-2-1-3.   Dawson Ty Riddiough, born 24 Feb 2008.

1-8-2-2.   Chantelle Riddough, born 25 Dec 1980. Married _____ Betts on 9 Jun 2007, but the marriage ended in divorce.   One child was:

1-8-2-2-1.   Dane Edward Betts, born 31 Oct 2008.

1-8-2-3.   Bradley Kevin Riddiough, born 10 Apr 1984.

1-8-2-3-1.   Dylan Rupert Riddiough, born 5 Jan 2009.

1-9. Unnamed infant McClaflin, born and died 1933.

2. George Wing Cissell, born Sep 1896 married Alma Isodore McCullough (born 27 May 1900) Apr 1920 in Haney, British Columbia, Canada. George died 11 Mar 1953 and Alma on 11 Mar 1984[73].

George Cissell and Alma McCullough in 1949.

---

[73] Both are buried at Maple Ridge Cemetery, Haney, BC.

They had two children:

2-1.   George Glenn Cissell, born 6 Nov 1922 in Ponoka married Cynthia Doreen Bertram) (born 25 Nov 1929, daughter of H. J. Bertram of Norwich, England on 20 Apr 1957 in Haney, BC. Cynthia died 9 April 2005. Their children included:

2-1-1.   Cynthia Doreen Cissell, born 13 Mar 1958 in Haney, BC[74]. Children included:

2-1-1-1. Michael _____, born 25 Apr 1982.

2-1-1-2. Ryan _____, born 3 May 1983.

2-1-2.   Raymond Glenn Cissell, born 7 Jan 1964 in Prince Rupert, BC was adopted by George and Cynthia.   Children associated with him include:

2-1-2-1. Samantha _____, born 14 Sep 1994.

2-1-1-1-1. Daughter born about Nov 2013.

2-1-2-2. Dyllan Cissell, born 9 Dec 1998

2-1-3.   Keith Wayne Cissell, born 11 Oct 1964 in Haney, BC. Married Nicole Pinchuck (born 1973) on 15 Jun 2007. Children include

2-1-3-1. Christian Cissell, born 14 Mar 1990.

2-1-3-2. Derrick Cissell.

2-1-4.   David George Cissell, born 2 Oct 1967 in Edmonton, Alberta.   Children from a first relationship (Marti Yakubow) include:

2-1-4-1. Amber Cissell, born 28 Apr 1988. Had a son:

[74] Doreen Cynthia Cissell was the first baby born in the then newly opened Maple Ridge Hospital in Port Haney.

2-1-4-1-1. Ty David _____, born 21 Dec 2011.

2-1-4-2. Jodi Cissell, born 11 Dec 1990. Jodi had at least two children:
2-1-4-2-1. Lian John ____, born 6 May 2009.

2-1-4-2-1. Myah _____, born about Sep 2012.

2-1-4-3. Torrie Cissell, born 20 Feb 1994.

2-1-4-4. Devon Cissell, born before 2000.

David had at least one other daughter from a second relationship:

2-1-4-5. Tristan Cynthia Cissell, born 11 Nov 1995.

2-2. Alma Marguerite Cissell, born 5 Jun 1925 in Ponoka, married Arthur Lemke (born 25 Apr 1918) on 14 Apr 1942 in Wetaskwin, AB. Alma died in 1961 and Arthur on 16 Feb 2002. Their children, all born in Ponoka included:

2-2-1. Leslie Robert Lemke, born 18 Jun 1943. Married Eileen McHugh. Their family included:

2-2-1-1. Belinda McHugh Lemke, born 21 Mar 1976. Married first Bill Lauzon on 18 May 1996. This marriage ended in divorce. Married secondly, Charles Thomas Krochak on 25 Jun 2011. Children included:

2-2-1-1-1. Tanner Evan Krochak, born 16 Aug 2011.

2-2-2. Vincent Duane Lemke, born 31 Jan 1946. Married Ruth Charters (born 11 May 1947) on 10 Oct 1970. Children were:

2-2-2-1. Dana Ruth Lemke, born 20 Dec 1971 in Kimberly, BC. Married Steven Roy Haller on 1 Jul 1995. Children included:

2-2-2-1-1. Kyran Rose Haller, born 21 Jun 1998.

2-2-2-1-2. Abigale Lynn Haller, born 22 Nov 1999.

2-2-2-1-2. Marrin Karolinea Haller, born 20 Dec 2001.

2-2-2-2. Duane Vincent Lemke, born 15 Jan 1973. Married Anita Korcoran on 22 June 2002. The couple separated, but had the following children:

2-2-2-2-1. Kayla Skye Lemke, born 8 Apr 2004

2-2-2-2-2. Karissa Page Lemke, born 5 Jul 2007.

2-2-3. Douglas Lemke, born 27 Dec 1950 in Ponoka. Married Margaret Cathro (born 21 Jan 1951) on 25 Jun 1971. Children were:

2-2-3-1. Shaun Lemke, born 15 Feb 1974. Married Sarah Glover on 8 May 2003. Children were:

2-2-3-1-1. Gabriella Reed Lemke, born 24 Apr 2006.

2-2-3-1-2. Connor Arthur Lemke, born 15 Nov 2010.

2-2-3-2. Cory Lemke, born Nov 1976. Married first Jodi Tomchyshyn on 26 Jul 2003. This marriage ended in divorce. Married Secondly Chelsa Gondek on 2 Jul 2011. Children included:

2-2-3-2-1. Declan Jude Lemke, born 23 May 2012.

2-2-4. Beverly Lemke, born 7 Nov 1953 married Clifford Bunney (born 10 Aug 1947) on 12 Jun 1971. Children included:

2-2-4-1. Laurie Bunney, born 17 Apr 1970.

2-2-4-2. Nicole Bunney, born 9 Aug 1972 in Whitecourt, AB. Married Jason Lee Batiuk (born 24 Oct 1978) on 6 Jun 2009. Children included:

2-2-4-2-1. Isadora Elizabeth Batiuk, born 6 Jul 2010.

2-2-4-2-2. Lucas James Batiuk, born 21 Aug 2012.

2-2-4-3. Shane Bunney, born 5 Jan 1976.

2-2-5. Kevin Lemke, born 20 Nov 1957. Partner was Suzanne Smid. Suzanne had a daughter, Danielle Smid.

3. Raymond C. Cissell was born about Aug 1903 in Ponoka. Died 26 Dec 1905. Buried at Dakota Cemetery.

4. Lodema Thelma Cissell, born 5 Sep 1905, married first Loring Marsh 24 Mar 1924. They had one child:

4-1. Opal Viaolla Marsh, born 18 Oct 1924 in Ponoka. Opal married first Frank Stewart (son of William Stewart and Ada Heath) in 1944. Their children included:

4-1-1. Stanley Stewart, born 18 Jun 1945.

4-1-2. Diane Stewart, born 20 Jul 1946.

4-1-3. Larry Stewart, born in 1948.

Opal married secondly, Kenneth Cunningham. Opal and Kenneth's children included:

4-1-4. Donald Cunningham.

4-1-5. Tommy Cunningham.

4-1-6. Sharon Cunningham.

Opal married thirdly, Ronald Thorne.

Lodema married second Ernest Dewey Allison in May 1931. Lodema and Ernest had the following children:

4-2. Carrie Emeline Allisen, born 6 Dec 1931 in Rimbey, Alberta. She married Ignace Frank Frey (born 12 Oct 1927 in Hungary) on 13 Jan 1951 at Oliver, BC. Their children included:

4-2-1. Shirley Ann Frey, born 8 May 1952 in Oliver, BC. She married Harold Fleck (born 4 Mar 1948) on 11 Nov 1970. Their children included:

4-2-1-1. Annette Christine Fleck, born 15 Jun 1971 in Calgary. Married Jason Richard Spalding (born 11 Feb 1970) on 17 Apr 1999.

4-2-1-2. Karen Ann Marie Fleck, born 26 May 1973 in Calgary. Married David Baillie on 18 Jul 2009. They had a son:

4-2-1-2-1. Nathan Baillie, born 9 Dec 2010.

4-2-2. Joseph Ernest Frey, born 4 Nov 1953 in Oliver, BC. Married Sue Ann Jessie Bales (born 25 Sep 1956) on 3 Sep 1977. They were divorced in 1983. Children were:

4-2-2-1. Shawna Lynn Frey, born 20 Jan 1978.

4-2-2-2. Kenneth Frank Frey, born 19 Aug 1979.

4-2-3. Richard Frank Frey, born 7 Feb 1955 in Oliver, BC. Richard married first Susan Dorothy Kozub (born 2 Jan 1956) on 8 Nov 1980. The marriage ended in divorce; Susan died 8 Feb 1997. Richard married secondly Sandra Lee Osborne (born 4 Jun 1961). Children included:

4-2-3-1. Natalie Janeil Frey, born 15 May 1990.

4-2-4. Sandra Kay Frey, born 17 Oct 1956 in Ponoka. Married David Dubbin (born 25 May 1956) on 24 May 1980. Children included:

4-2-4-1. David Ernest Dubbin, born 24 Mar 1985.

4-2-4-2. Jason Frank Dubbin, born 21 Feb 1988.

4-2-5. Donald George Frey, born 2 Sep 1959 in Calgary. Married Jocelyn _____ (born 19 Jul 1960) on 25 Jul 1982. Children included:

4-2-5-1. Kaitlynn Avonne Frey, born 23 Jul 1992.

4-2-5-1. Camille Paige Frey, born 25 May 1995.

4-3. Gertrude Lodema Allison, born 23 Jul 1936 in Ponoka. She married Joseph Lawrence Prefontaine (born 22 Mar 1936) on 4 Aug

1956. Joseph had been adopted by Charles Prefontaine and his wife Rose. Joseph died 4 Aug 2010. Their children, born in Calgary, Alberta, included:

4-3-1. Edward Charles Prefontaine, born 5 May 1957. Married Marilyn Elaine Olsen (born 24 Jun 1958) on 11 Mar 1977. Marilyn died 13 Jun 1977.

4-3-2. Patrick Ernest Prefontaine, born 6 Aug 1958. Married Andrea Joyce Constable (born 22 Sep 1961) on 26 Aug 1989. Children were:

> 4-3-2-1. Matthew William Joseph Prefontaine, born 15 Dec 1992.

> 4-3-2-2. Mariea Nicole Prefontaine, born 15 Aug 1994.

> 4-3-2-3. Kathryn Elizabeth Prefontaine, born 8 Dec 1997.

4-3-3. James Allan Prefontaine, born 19 Sep 1959. Died 11 Jan 1978.

4-3-4. Carolyn Thelma Mary Prefontaine, born 20 Sep 1960. Married first Brian Malley on 23 Oct 1976. Married secondly, Derik Lane. Married thirdly, Robert Murray Dixon (born 2 Dec 1956) on 2 Feb 1991. Children included:

> 4-3-4-1. Jennifer Malley, born 1 Apr 1977. Married Brian Wayne McLellan (born 19 Aug 1970) on 29 Apr 2000. Children included:

>> 4-3-4-1-1. Joshua Robert McLellan, born 8 Apr 2002

>> 4-3-4-1-2. Kristin Jade McLellan, born 12 Jul 2005.

>> 4-3-4-1-3. Liam Joseph McLellan, born 4 Jan 2008.

> 4-3-4-2. Kyle James Alexander Lane, born 13 Mar 1983. Married Tanya Nicole Mason (born 9 Mar 1984) on 13 Aug 2005. Children included:

>> 4-3-4-2-1. Erek Alexander Lane, born 29 Oct 2001.

>> 4-3-4-2-2. Kaden Lane.

4-3-4-3. Jamie Michael Lane, born 18 Jun 1984.

4-3-5. David Lawrence Prefontaine, born 16 Mar 1966 in Calgary. Married Natalie Ann Saunders (born 22 Mar 1967) on 22 Jul 2000. Children included:

4-3-5-1. Jessica Michele Prefontaine, born 9 Jun 2001.

4-3-6. Faye Marie Prefontaine, born 5 Apr 1968. Married Shawn Michael Craven (born 16 Jun1967) on 30 Jun 1990. Children included:

4-3-6-1. Allison Jeanette Craven, born 29 Aug 1995.

4-3-6-2. Erica Rose Craven, born 23 Aug 1998.

4-4. George Dale Allison (the nephew of Ernest Dewey Allison), had been born 23 May 1937 and was adopted by Lodema and Ernest. He married Margaret Anne Evans (born 9 Jun 1968) on 16 Sep 2000.

5. Emma Lottie Cissell[75], born 17 Feb 1910. Married Milton Rockwell Olmstead (born 9 Nov 1904) on 26 Dec 1931.

It took a lot to work a farm. Emma provided the following memory:

> "...... Another thing I learned was, that it was easier to learn to drive four horses on the binder than to stook the bundles in the field (my husband co-op'd here). However it was necessary to watch that you always dropped the bundles in a straight row for the stooker (or you would be told). The threshing crew were not very happy when they were pitching those bundles into the hayrack, to take to the threshing machine if they had to zig-zag all over the field.[76]"

Emma and Milton continued the blueberry picking traditions of Emma's parents. In late Jul 1946 their crops were ruined by a hailstorm. In the middle of August they went looking for blueberries, north of Springdale, about 25-30 miles from their home. They had a Ford truck and since they

---

[75] Some of her family history is covered in her book, "Roots of Wings".

[76] The process for harvesting grain involved using a binder machine to cut and tie the plants into bundles. Several of these bundles were then hand-stooked (set up together on end) to dry in the field. Crews then pitched the bundles into a hayrack that took them to the threshing machine to separate out the grain.

had no crop left to worry about they spent much time picking the berries; the ground was just blue with them. They got all they needed the first day and so took some the Co-Op[77] in Ponoka. They were offered 30 cents per pound if they took credit instead of cash. This seemed like a good offer and they decided to try picking some more. Milton made little pickers for their daughter Louise (about 11 yrs) and son Kenneth (about 8 yrs). They told them they could have all the money they could make.

They got up early to do the chores[78] and then tried to start picking about 10:30 if there wasn't too much dew. They took their dinner and super along, as well as a snack. They picked for two days and cleaned them on the third. They put up two flannelette blankets on two poles and leaned them on the double wagon box of the Ford. At the bottom Emma put some sheets to hold the berries, then stood on top and poured the berries slowly down the blanket. The leaves blew out and they were clean when they reached the bottom. They took them to town that same day. Louise averaged about $7 per day, and Kenneth about $4. The money went a long ways then. Sugar was about $4.50 per hundred pounds; flour about $2.80 per hundred pounds; and coffee 40 cents per pound. They stocked up and had plenty of credit left over.

The Co-Op had a case of wool left over from the year before. It was grey and white and there was not much demand for it. Emma bought it at a much-reduced price. By the middle of September their crop had come back quite well so they got a good crop of oats, some light barley and plenty of greenfeed, enough to carry them through the winter. When the winter set in, Emma got out her knitting machine and started knitting men's socks. She made enough for the family, but still had lots of the wool left over. She took some into the Co-Op and they offered $1.30 for each pair she could make. She could make about 11 or 12 pair a day; earning not quite as much as picking blueberries, but the work was not as hard. As a result, the year with the hail damage wasn't as bad as it might have been.

Emma did much to help record her family history. She provided significant inputs for the Cissell section in Timothy J. O'Rourke's "*Maryland Catholics on the Frontier*" in 1973. She also created her book, "*The Roots of Wings*"[79] in 1985 to document the David Wing family.

---

[77] Then known as United Farmers of Alberta (U.F.A.).

[78] They were milking 10 to 12 cows, had pigs, chickens and turkeys. The milk was separated by hand and the cream could be sold for as much as $4.00 per 8-gallon can.

[79] Emma's document contains photos of many of the individuals in this Chapter and so they are not duplicated here.

Milton died 6 Sep 1977. Emma died 18 Apr 2012 in Ponoka, at age 102. In addition to adopting Juanita Betty Kessler, their children included:

5-1. Inez Louise Olmstead, born 11 Oct 1935 in Ponoka. Married Ronald Percy Doupe (born 17 Jun 1929) on 17 Nov 1956. Ronald was the son of Percy Doupe and Lila Johnson. Inez died 1 Nov 1993 and Ronald on 23 Mar 2007. Their children, all born in Ponoka included:

> 5-1-1. Ronald Lynn Doupe, born 3 Oct 1957. Married Kim Gore (born 28 Aug 1957) on 20 Apr 1985. The marriage ended in divorce. In addition to Ronald's stepson, Casey Gore (born 12 Mar 1978), their children included:

>> 5-1-1-1. Chelsea Dawn Doupe, born 6 Aug 1986.

>> 5-1-1-2. Breanne Louise Doupe, born 30 Jun 1988.

> 5-1-2. Edwin Wesley Doupe, born 26 Oct 1959. Married Lise Runtie (born 24 Mar 1959) on 10 Nov 1984. Children included:

>> 5-1-2-1. Evan Marshall Doupe, born 29 Dec 1987.

>> 5-1-2-2. Braden Tyler Doupe, born 30 Oct 1991.

>> 5-1-2-3. Lauryn Candice Doupe, born 15 Sep 1993.

> 5-1-3. Pearl Louise Doupe, born 19 Jun 1961.

> 5-1-4. Trent Ernest Doupe, born 28 May 1964. Married Joanne Caroline Henkelman (born 14 Jul 1963) on 21 Nov 1992. Children included:

>> 5-1-4-1. Sam Milton Doupe, born 8 Jan 1994.

>> 5-1-4-2. Louise Caroline Doupe, born 24 Aug 1995.

5-2. Kenneth Darrell Olmstead, born 15 Dec 1938 in Ponoka. Married first Donna Gayle Phillips (born 3 Dec 1944, the daughter of William Phillips and Pauline Betts) in July 1965 at Ponoka Baptist Church. The marriage ended in divorce. Kenneth married secondly, Leona (Fluet) Irvine (born 3 Sep 1936) on 11 Oct 1981. Leona died 23 Jul 1998 and Kenneth on 13 Sep 2010.

5-3. Donna Marie Olmstead was born 21 Feb 1948. She married Richard Nicolas Street on 2 Jul 1966 at the Ponoka United Church. Nicolas was born 19 Apr 1946 and was the son of Richard John Street and Hazel Arlene Johnson. Their children included:

5-3-1. Sandra Marie Street, born 25 Sep 1968 in Ponoka. Sandra married Douglas Owen John Lund on 27 Aug 1994. Douglas was born 3 Dec 1958. Their children included:

5-3-1-1. Alexandria Marie Lund, born 13 Jan 1997.

5-3-2. Katherine Ross Street, born 29 Jul 1970 in Ponoka. Married Bradley Olsen (born 3 Aug 1965) on 14 Sep 2002. This marriage ended with divorce in 2005. Children were:

5-3-2-1. Steven Bradley Olsen, born 18 Sep 1997.

5-3-2-2. Emma Rose Olsen, born 12 Apr 2004.

6. Walter Merl Cissell, born 13 Aug 1914 in Ponoka, married Hilda Irma Mass (born 1 Mar 1921) on 29 Jun 1941. Walter died 13 Mar 1984 and Hilda on 23 Jul 2009. Children included:

6-1. Judy Cissell, born 24 Feb 1943, Ponoka. She married Jerry Raymond Miller (born 21 Aug 1942) on 11 Jul 1964 in Ponoka. Jerry was the son of Harry Miller and Mrytle Schmolund. Jerry worked at the B.A. oil plant facility; Judy taught at Ponoka and Crestomere schools. They were divorced in Aug 1991. Jerry died 10 Sep 1996. Judy married secondly, Merle Jones (born 10 Aug 1939) on 22 May 2001. Judy's children were:

6-1-1. Mark Gregory Miller, born 8 Aug 1972 in Ponoka. Married Pamela Dawn Anderson (born 12 Nov 1974) on 28 Aug 2010. Pamela had one daughter:

6-1-1-1. Jamecia Dawn Anderson-Miller, born 25 Nov 1995.

6-1-2. Gregory Mark Miller, born 14 Jul 1974. Married Jolene Nicole Larson (born 25 Feb 1974) on 21 Feb 2006. Children include:

6-1-2-1. Nate Micah Miller, born 12 Nov 2007.

6-1-2-2. Neriah May Miller, born 17 Jul 2009.

6-2. Elaine Ann Cissell, born 1 Aug 1945 in Ponoka, married Richard Alfred Groom on 24 Sep 1966 in Ponoka. Richard had been born 1 Mar 1945 and was the son of Alfred and Gladys Groom. Children, all born in Red Deer, Alberta, included:

6-2-1. Monica Elaine Groom, born 14 Jul 1969. Married Jeffery James Harvey (born 28 Nov 1969) on 14 Aug 1993. Children included:

6-2-1-1. Jonah Lewis Harvey, born 27 Oct 1995.

6-2-1-2. Virginia Lane Harvey, born 1 May 1997.

6-2-1-3. Julianna Grace Harvey, born 29 Mar 2000.

6-2-2. Ronald Richard Groom, born 15 Apr 1972. Died 14 Nov 1998.

6-3. Frank David Cissell, born 19 Apr 1947 married Patricia Anne Palechek on 7 Jul 1967. Patricia was born 15 Feb 1946. Their children included:

6-3-1. Chad David Cissell, born 29 Sep 1969. Chad married Alana Johnson (born 8 Jul 1969) on 3 Apr 1992. Their children included:

6-3-1-1. Erika Ann Cissell, born 26 Oct 1994.

6-3-1-2. Bret Charles Cissell, born 21 Dec 1997.

6-3-2. Chantelle Patricia Cissell, born 4 May 1972. Married Darren Godfrey (born 29 Jun 1969) on 22 Jun 2002. Children included:

6-3-2-1. Logan Chistopher Godfrey, born 7 May 2003.

6-3-2-2. Jordan Emily Godfrey, born 2 Mar 2005.

Chad Cissell, Bret Cissell, Patricia Palechek , Logan Godfrey, Jordan Godfrey, Frank Cissell, and David Cissell in 2014.

6-4. Connie Cora Cissell, born 31 May 1953 married Bryan Ross Pretula. Bryan was born 18 Nov 1953. Their children included:

6-4-1. Leanne Connie Pretula, born 1 Aug 1977.

6-4-2. Steven Bryan Pretula, born 6 Nov 1981. Steven married Crystal Marie Derouin (born 1 Mar 1981) on 25 Jul 2009. Their children include:

6-4-2-1. Peyton John Louis Pretula, born 12 Dec 2010.

6-4-2-2. Paisley Marie Pretula, born 10 Dec 2012.

Two of Frank's sisters Alice, and Etta had died in SD prior to the family's move to Ponoka. His sister Emma, had come to Ponoka but eventually returned to SD as well. The stories of these three sisters are provided in the next Chapter.

7. South Dakota
Alice, Etta, and Emma Cissell

Alice L. Cissell, daughter of Nerius Cissell and Alice Mary Bey, was born 1 Jun 1875 in Westfield, Dodge County, Minnesota. She married Richard J. Mueller (Muller) about 1894. Richard had been born 5 Jul 1867[80] in Wisconsin. The 1900 US Census shows them living next door to her parents in Oldham, Kingsbury County, South Dakota. Richard's occupation at that time was given as grain buyer. The census showed they had an adopted son, Ray C. Mueller, born February 1900, but no natural children. Alice died the following year, 29 Mar 1901 and so had no children. Richard remarried, Mary Margaret Bloom (born about 1883 IA), on 26 August 1903. Richard and Mary had at least one daughter, Myrtle M. Mueller, born about 1906 in South Dakota.  They lived for a while in North Dakota but eventually returned to South Dakota. In 1931, for example, they were at 508 Fourth St., Madison, SD. Alice (also identified in cemetery records as Alice L. Sicol) is buried in Graceland Cemetery, Lot 14, at Madison, Lake County, South Dakota. Richard died 22 September 1958 and is buried in the same cemetery. Richard's second wife, Mary (4 Dec 1883 - 7 January 1960), is also buried at the Graceland Cemetery. In 1940 Ray Mueller, and his wife Virginia, were living at 2420 California St. in Denver CO.

Etta M. Cissell, daughter of Nerius Cissell and Alice Mary Bey, was born ca. 1869 in Ashland Township, Dodge County, MN. She married W. F. Davis (born IA), probably in 1889. They had one son, Frank Daniels Davis, who was born 11 Mar 1890[81] in Madison, Lake County, SD. Nerius's pension application forms imply that Etta died sometime before 1898 (and

---

[80] Some Graceland Cemetery records claim a birth date of 1861, but this does not agree with census records.

[81] This birth date is taken from his Canadian military "Attestation Paper" which he signed on 31 May 1916. This differs from that indicated on his South Dakota death record.

so possibly as early as 1890).   By 1900, Frank was living with his Grandparents, Nerius and Alice Cissell.

On May 31 1916, at Lacombe, Alberta, Frank Daniels Davis enlisted with the Canadian Over-Seas Expeditionary Force, 211th Battalion (American Legion) and was assigned a Regiment, or military serial number of 258363. His papers described him as Dark complexioned, with Blue eyes and Black hair and as a Baptist. He was 5ft 11inches tall and weighed 140 lbs. His Canadian military records end on 16 October 1916, shortly before the Battalion was to be sent overseas. On that date he is recorded as being a "Deserter".

Frank, however, did then "re-enlist" in the United States on 4 Jun 1917. He served with Company C, 116th Supply Train of the 41st Division. The 41st was made up from the National Guards of Washington, Oregon, Montana, Utah, and Wyoming at Camp Greene, NC. It arrived in France by 7 Dec 1917 and remained active there until at least 31 Dec 1918. Frank was discharged with the rank of Corporal on 15 Feb 1919.

Frank and his wife, Mary B. _____, were married about 1919. They had one daughter, Emalyne M. Davis, born 19 Sep 1920 possibly in ND[82]. She married Harvey W. Brooksmith (ca 1918 - 10 Sep 1976). Emalyne died 8 Mar 1992 in Cheyenne, WY and is buried at Bethel Cemetery there (Sec M, Lot 75, Space D). Emalyne had three sons:

    1. Harvey William "Bill" Brooksmith, born 17 Jun 1942. Died 23 Aug 1985, WY. (Married Susan "Sue" ____ (1947-1988)). Harvey died in a vehicle accident.

    2.   Douglas J. Brooksmith, born 19 Jul 1949. Died 31 Oct 1993, Laramie, WY. Married _____. Children included:

        2-1. Douglas J. Brooksmith.

    3. Terry Brooksmith.

Frank died in Huron, Beadle County, SD on 19 Aug 1939, and was buried in Arlington Cemetery, Arlington, Brookings County, SD on 23 Aug 1939 (Block 4, Lot 17, Grave 13).

---

[82] It is noted that "Emalyne" (or "Emaline") was the middle name of Frank's Aunt, Cora E. Cissell.

Emma Rose Cissell, daughter of Nerius Cissell and Alice Mary Bey was born about 25 Aug 1883 in Ashland Township, Dodge County, Minnesota.

She married first Emil Marius Wold [83] [84], prior to Feb 1902. Emil had been born 22 Jun 1878 in Stokmarknes, Norway. He served with the US Army in the Philippines during the Spanish American War. He was considered handsome and "all the girls chased him". On his wedding night, one woman who thought he had been going to marry her, had Emil jailed for breach of promise; and he spent that night in jail.

In 1902 Emil applied for a homestead on the land just east of Nerius Cissell's property near Ponoka. On 21 Jun 1905, Emil was granted Canadian Citizenship by the Supreme Court of the North West Territories. He then seems to have returned to the States and to Volga, SD. From Volga, in Mar 1906 he told the Department of the Interior that he had leased his homestead land for 1 year to L. A. Cissell. The leasing of homestead land was not normally legal and should have caused forfeiture of his homestead. But in Apr 1906, the Deputy Minister of the Interior wrote,

> "...There is nothing, however, on file to indicate that Mr. Wold gave this lease with any intention of fraud or injury to the Crown, and I, therefore, beg to recommend that the forfeiture of his homestead, the said S.E. 1/4 of Section 16, Township 47, Range 27, West Fourth Meridian, be waived."

It is not clear what the final resolution of this problem was, but a patent for the land was issued to Emil on 12 Jun 1906 and at which time he was still living in Volga, SD.

He does not seem to have returned to Canada; neither he nor Emma is mentioned in the 1906 census of Alberta. By the 1910 census, Emma seemed to be working as a servant with a family in Wasco, OR and Emil was not living with her. They then appear to have divorced, as both remarried in 1918.

[83] Maryland Catholics on the Frontier, 1973, Timothy J. O'Rourke, p. 519.

[84] Edmonton Bulletin newspaper, 10 Feb 1902, p. 6.

Emil remarried Hazel Frances Schuster, a divorcee with two children, on 18 Nov 1918 in Hardin, MT[85]. Hazel was the daughter of Alfred Nelson and Margaret Francis. Emil and Hazel were musically inclined and both could play the violin. They played for dances and silent movies in Wyoming and Nebraska from 1918 to 1924 and continued to play in Southern California into the mid-1930s. Emil died 3 Apr 1945 and was buried as "Amil Marius Wold" at the Los Angeles National Cemetery.

The Aberdeen American newspaper in South Dakota recorded Emma's second marriage, several months prior to Emil's, on 13 Jun 1918:

> "Deadwood – Miss Emma Weld and Edward B. Kenley of Volga , were united in marriage at the home of Mr. and Mrs. J. W. Fowler, 115 Charles Street , by Rev. J. Maurice Hupp. Mr. and Mrs. Kenley will make their future home at Volga where he is a builder and contractor."

A 1909 business directory [86] also associated Ed. B. Kenly with a restaurant in Volga South Dakota.

Emma Cissell and Edward Kenly:

Two Emma's[87]:

Emma Cissell Olmstead with her aunt,
Emma Cissell Kenly.

Edward Kenly (Nov 1887 - 3 Jan 1940) is buried at First Lutheran Cemetery, Volga, SD in Lot 24-3, Grave 10. His mother, Andria E. Kenly, (1857 - 1912) is also buried there in Lot 24-3, Grave 12.

Family letters show that Emma Kenly was living in Volga, SD in 1947. She married thirdly, Hans Christian Kalberg. Hans was born 26 Apr 1879 in South Dakota and died there 1 Mar 1948. Hans was buried in the First Lutheran Cemetery, Volga, SD. next to his first wife, Cecilia O. Kalberg, who had died 20 Jun 1930. Emma died 30 Aug 1950 and is buried as "Emma R. Kalberg" at the First Lutheran Cemetery in lot 24-3, Grave 8[88] and so next to her husband, Edward B. Kenly. No children are known.

---

[87] Copy of a photo from Judy Cissell Miller Jones.
[88] [44.313278,-96.92871]

8. Yakima, Washington
Leon Albert Cissell's Family

Alice Mary Bey left Pokoka and returned to the United States in 1919. She settled in Yakima, Washington. Almost all of the children of her son Leon also came to Yakima. Her daughter Bessie (Bailey) and her family came as well. This and the next chapter provide the stories of Leon and Bessie and their Yakima branches of the family.

Leon (Leo) Albert Cissell[89], son of Nerius Cissell and Alice Mary Bey, was born in Ashland Township, Dodge County, Minnesota about 29 Jun 1867. He married Clara May Thorsness in Kingsbury County SD about 1892.

Leon Cissell and Clara Thorsness with a son (probably William Cissell)

---

[89] On documents, Leon signed his name as "Leo A. Cissell".

Clara, born May 1876 in MN, was the daughter of Servert Thorsness and Ulrikka M. Norman. Severt and Ulrika had been born in Norway and settled in Vallers Township (Section 28), Lyon County, MN. Severt had likely been born 8 Jan 1847 near the Thorsness Farm in Balestrand County, Norway on the north side of the longest fiord in the country[90] . His father was Hans (ca 1820) and his mother Britha (ca 1825). Ulrikka came from Sund, near Buksnes, Gravdal, Norway[91]. Ulrikka's father was John Peter and her mother, Marthe (Martha). Her siblings, all born in Norway, but whom moved to the US included:

Aletta C. Norman	(1849 - 22 Oct 1889, MN)
Johanna Norman	(1854 -)
Jennie Norman?	(1853/1857? -)
Arndt S. Norman	(26 Mar 1859 - 7 Dec 1900, MN)
Franz Norman	(Jun 1862 -)

Servert and Ulrikka were married about 1874 in Minnesota. By 1900 they were living in Mankato, MN. They then moved to OR. Ulrikka died 13 Apr 1917 in Portland, OR and Servert died there on 13 Jan 1922. They are buried together at the Milwaukie Pioneer Cemetery near Portland[92] and near two of their children, Henry B. and Selmer V. Servert and Ulrikka's children included:

Henry O. Thorsness (7 Jan 1875, MN -   )
Clara M. Thorsness (1876, MN - 11 Sep 1913, Alberta)
Emma Christina Thorness[93] (4 Apr 1877, MN - Aug 1966, Los Angeles, CA)
John O. Thorsness   (Apr 1882, MN - 11 Oct 1944, CA)
Henry B. Thorsness   (Apr 1884, MN - 29 Sep 1924, OR)
Selmer V. Thorsness (Feb 1888, SD - 13 Aug 1914, OR)
Elmer E. Thorsness   (Nov 1891, SD - OR)
Mabel Marie Thorsness[94] (Apr 1894, SD - 26 Oct 1932, Los Angeles, CA)

---

[90] [61.274193, 6.5442]

[91] [68.113302, 13.484503]

[92] Samuel H. Thorsness and Ulricka M. Thorsness are buried in Plot 40, Spaces 2 and 1. Henry B. is in Plot 40, Space 8. Selmer V. is in Plot 41, Space 4. Approximate location is [45.453483, -112.647135]. The family did not provide markers for any of them.

[93] Married first Andrew LaFontaine (1843, Canada - before 1930, OR). Married 2nd Edward Rogers, before 1937.

[94] Married William J. Fasching (25 Mar 1892 - 2 Oct 1961) on 16 Aug 1924. Death date is from a family letter of Emma (Thorsness) LaFontaine to Claud Cissell on 18 Dec 1932.

Leon Cissell and Clara May Thorsness had 9 known children [95]:

1. William Arthur "Bill" Cissell. Born 14 Feb 1893[96], Oldham, SD. Died 19 Apr 1960, Ellensburg, WA[97]. In Ponoka, Bill worked on the family farm and in 1916 was a servant for the neighboring Lesley V. Bailey[98], family. Bill worked as a carpenter after coming to Yakima in the early 1920's.

He married Dora V. Emerson (17 Jun 1905-7 Jul 2006) on 28 May 1933 in Ellensburg, WA. They had met at a family dance in 1924. They were photographed as a couple (on the right), at the wedding of Dora's sister Vida to Emil Leo Bapst on 3 Dec 1927 and signed together as the witnesses on the marriage certificate. William continued his construction career in Ellensburg as a builder. Dora[99] was a well-known educator; she had first taught in a one-room country school in eastern Montana and then in Ellensburg and in Japan and Germany for the Department of Defense. Bill and Dora had no children.

2. Ernest L. "Dutch"[100] Cissell. Born 3 Jan 1897, Oldham, SD. Died 5 February 1965, Olympia, WA. (Continued.)

3. Claud Richard "Ole"[101] Cissell. Born 5 Dec 1898, Oldham, SD. Died 14 Oct 1965, Tillicum, WA. (Continued.)

---

[95] The 1900 SD census lists 3 sons (William A., Ernest L., & Claude R.). The form also indicates that Clara had had 4 children, but with just 3 still living. It is not clear who that 4th child was {it may have been Grace, who died young}. The census form also indicates that Leon and Clara had been married for 8 years and so implies that they were married about 1892.

[96] William Cissell's birth date is indicated as being 1893 in census records for 1900 (SD), 1906 (Alberta), and 1920 (SD). The birth certificate that that was later created for him in SD also has this date. On the other hand, the 1940 (WA) census and Washington State death records indicate that he was born in 1896. The 1893 date appears to be correct and will be used here.

[97] He and his wife are buried in the IOOF Cemetery in Ellensburg. Plot H-040-08.

[98] Lesley was one of Clinton D. Bailey's brothers and so a brother-in-law to Bessie Cissell.

[99] {On a personal note, Dora had a rough, raspy voice.}

[100] The nickname "Dutch" could possibly have come from Ernest's card playing, but the actual origin is not known.

4. Albert Lewis "Jim" Cissell. Born ca. 1901, Oldham, SD. Died 26 Apr 1945, Seattle, WA. (Continued.)

5. Alice Cissell. Born ca 1904, probably Oldham, SD. Died 8 Jan 1906, Ponoka, Alberta, age 2.

6. Harry Norman Cissell. Born 27 May 1907, Ponoka, Alberta. Died 27 Sep 1982, Olympia, WA. (Continued.)

7. Vera Chrystell "Pat" Cissell. Born 5 Jul 1910, Ponoka, Alberta. She returned to the United States at about age 6, on 25 Feb 1916 (7 months after the death of her father), going by rail through Sweetgrass, MT. She seems to have been sent to stay with her aunt Emma (Cissell) Kenly in Volga, SD. She, and her brother William Cissell were there with Emma for the 1920 census. Vera remained in Volga through at least 1925.

Although all of Vera's brothers were in Yakima, WA by the early 1920s they still acted as a family and helped as best they could. It is not known exactly what was going on with Vera at this time, but a family letter, written 25 April 1927, gives some information. It was from William Cissell to his brother Claud:

"

Ellensburg Wash.
April 25

Dear Bro.

Rec'd your letter in regard to Vera. Have you wrote to Emma[102] to see what she thinks about it? I know it is no place for her there. To many ruff necks. Now listen here when we send money we will send it to Emma, even tho' she is our sister. I believe it would be better to send it to her as she would know more what to do with it. As I think she has Dutche's

---

[101] The origins of the nickname "Ole" are also not known. However Claud did (correctly) consider himself to be of Norwegian descent. It is also noted that an "Ole" E. Thorsness lived near Oldham, SD in 1900 and could well have been a relative of Claud's mother.

[102] It's not clear if this is Vera's aunt, Emma (Cissell) Kenly in Volga SD or her aunt, Emma (Thorsness) Lafontaine in Portland OR. {Best guess, however, would be Emma Lafontaine.}

tricks. I know I should not say these things, but when they are true, I can't help it. So write to her - find out what she will take to keep her. I'll pay the tuition at school. Does she want to go to school. I'll tell you drive up some nite & bring her along so we can talk it over. Any nite but Wed.

I am Your Bro.
(Bill)"

Likely related to this issue is a 15 June 1927 telegram from Vera's aunt, Emma (Thorsness) Lafontaine in Portland Oregon to Vera's brother Claud then at 621 South 15 Ave, Yakima saying, "Vera will arrive by Stage[103] 615 PM". At that time, Vera would have been almost 17. She then seems to have stayed in Yakima. She was in school in Yakima from at least Oct 1927 through Jul 1928. In 1930 she was living with her brother Albert and his wife, Dollie. Vera married Gilbert Edward Greder (14 Sep 1910, CA - 25 Dec 1994, Quartsite, AZ) on 6 Mar 1933 in Ellensburg, WA.

After their marriage, Claud tried to help Gilbert and Vera in purchasing some land near Gromore[104] that was being sold for $2500. On 14 March 1933, he provided the deed for his house at 621 15th Ave. S., Yakima for the $700 down payment they needed to purchase the property. It appears, though, that the sale was not completed. Vera and Gilbert were still living in Yakima in 1940, but later moved to Olympia, WA.

In 1947 "Pat" and "Gil" started a hobby store in downtown Olympia called appropriately, "Chrystell's". The store never held sales, so near Christmastime their nieces and nephews received lots of the toy items that might

PAT AND GIL GREDER
Invite You to Celebrate

CHRYSTELL'S
GIFTS   TOYS   HOBBIES

13th Anniversary
OPEN HOUSE
April 13th through 16th, 1960

415 CAPITOL WAY
OLYMPIA, WASHINGTON

---

[103] That is by bus.
[104] N1/2 of SE1/4 of NW1/2 of Section 28, Township 13 N, Range 17 East of the Willamette Meridian, a bit SW of William Holden's farm.

otherwise have been sold at discount. As a hobby, "Gil" also operated a small gold mining claim (the Oro Fino Mine[105]) near Liberty, WA. They had no children, but did maintain some good Filbert trees!

In the late 1960's they decided that instead of spending money on health insurance, they would put aside $10,000 to pay for any medical problems that might occur. Unfortunately, Vera later suffered a stroke and the care needed for her well exceeded that amount. Vera died 15 Oct 1972 at a care facility in Centralia, WA.

8. Grace Cissell. Died young - possibly in SD, but actual date and location is not known.

9. Clarence Arthur Cissell. Born 26 Aug 1913, Ponoka, Alberta. Died 8 May 1984, Vancouver, BC. Clarence was just a baby at his mother's death and was too young for the remaining family to properly care for him. Accordingly, he was adopted by William A. Beacock and his wife Catherine L. The Beacocks had three older children, Aletta (1904); Emma (1908); Edward E. (1910) and like Frank and Cora Cissell were Saturday Adventists. Clarence used the "Beacock" name throughout his

life. He is buried in the Mountain View Cemetery, Vancouver, BC, Canada (Plot: HORNE2/*/05/*/0679)[106].

As mentioned above, Leon had made claim for a homestead on the SE 1/4 of Section 16, Township 43, Range 27, West of the 4th Meridian and next to his father's property on 22 Feb 1901. Like his father, he then had trouble selling his property in Oldham. On 25 Jul 1901 from Oldham, he wrote to the Department of the Interior to request an extension on his homestead, "... as it is impossible for me to sell my property here." The Canadian Government did not approve his extension request and cancelled his

---

[105] Located at approximately: [47.25872, -120.69867]. And there is gold there.

[106] Cissell family members provided a marker for Clarence's grave in 2012. (Its location is: [49.242272,-123.094149]) The initials in the lower right corner of the marker refer to the first names of those members: David Cissell, Julie Zalikowski, Lucia Thede, Stephen Cissell, and Victor Cissell.

homestead application on 7 Jul 1902. Leon's brother-in-law, Emil Wold, then took up the homesteading for that property. It was not until 1904 or 1905 that Leon was able to sell his property in Oldham and finally get to Ponoka to be with the rest of the family. Once there he leased the property back from Emil who then returned to the States.

In addition to initially leasing the land next to his parents, Leon applied for another homestead about 30 May 1906. This property was the NE 1/4 of Section 21, Township 44, Range 28, West of the 4th Meridian. On 29 Apr 1910 he was granted a patent for this land. As part of the application paperwork for the patent, the Government also certified, on 18 Mar 1910, that Leon had owned the land on the SE 1/4 of Section 16, Township 47, Range 27, West of the 4th Meridian (next to his mother's place) since 14 Aug 1906, when it had been registered.

Clara and Leon farmed the properties and lived with their family on the farm next door to Nerius and Alice. Their home as it appeared in the early 1970's. It was insulated with newspaper and pages taken from Sears catalogs:

Leon's wife, Clara Thorsness, died of typhoid fever on 11 Sep 1913, about 4 months after their son Clarence had been born.   Leon then left the farm and went to Medicine Hat where he managed the Factory Hotel (& Saloon) at 1028 Foundry Street. The remaining family members made their home with Grandma Cissell (Alice Bey) who still lived in the grey tin-sided house next door.

Leon died 3 Jul 1915 in Bismark (the Dakota District), Alberta, (most likely at his or his mother's home) reportedly from Typhoid Fever[107]. Leon and Clara are buried together, next to their daughter Alice, at the nearby Dakota United Cemetery[108]:

2. Ernest Leon "Dutch"[109] Cissell, the son of Leon Albert Cissell and Clara May Thorsness was born 3 Jan 1897[110], in Oldham, SD. He died 5 Feb 1965 in Olympia, WA. He married Lois Holloway on 2 Nov 1928 in Seattle, WA. Lois, the daughter of Francis (Frank) and Mabel A. Holloway, was born 10 Feb 1904 in Oregon and died 21 Feb 2002 in Olympia, WA. In addition to having worked on the family farm near Ponoka as a youth, and as a servant for the neighboring Charley Crandall family near Ponoka in 1916, Ernest was a steamfitter and plumber. By 1931 he was living at 110 2nd Ave N. in Yakima and working as a steamfitter with the plumbing firm, Milton

---

[107] His son Claud remembered seeing a black spot on Leon's hand before his death, but this is not normally a symptom of Typhoid Fever.

[108] Approximate location: [52.732973, -113.847883].

[109] The nickname "Dutch" could possibly have come from Ernest's card playing, but the actual origin is not known.

[110] Ernest's birth date is often given as 3 Jan 1898. However, the 1 Jun 1900 census of Oldham SD records his age as 3 and his birth date as Jan 1897. Generally census records closer to a person's birth should be more accurate than those taken later in life. The 12 Jul 1906 Alberta census gives his age as 9, which would suggest an even earlier date of 1896. Also the birth date of his next younger brother, Claud, was 5 Dec 1898. Accordingly, the date of 3 Jan 1897 is considered most likely to be correct and is used for this book. His grave marker displays the Jan 3, 1898 date.

Morton. The family moved to Olympia, WA some time after 1935; possibly in 1939. Ernest and Lois had two children:

2-1. Richard Lee "Dick" Cissell, born 16 Sep 1930 in Yakima, WA and died 17 May 2006 in Olympia, WA. He married Nelda Ann Bracy (1 May 1940, Olympia). Nelda was the daughter of Lucian A. and Catherine A. Bracy. He and Nelda had 3 children:

2-1-1. Leann Marie Cissell, born 28 Jan 1962 in Olympia, WA. She married Frank Anthony Caranci (26 Mar 1948, Philadelphia, PA). Leann and Anthony had 3 children:

2-1-1-1. Samantha Paige Caranci, born 16 Jul 1996 in Olympia, WA.

2-1-1-2. Daniel Anthony Michael Caranci, born 15 Aug 1998 in Olympia, WA.

2-1-1-3. Ivy Marie Caranci, born 16 Jun 1999 in Olympia, WA.

2-1-2. Lorie Jean Cissell, born 17 Feb 1963, Olympia, WA.

2-1-3. Lucia Ernestine Cissell, born 12 Jan 1970 in Olympia, WA. She married Lennie E. Thede (6 Dec 1971, Olympia, WA) on 8 Apr 2000. Their son Luca Alexander Thede was born 30 Oct 2006 in Olympia, WA.)

2-3. Lois Jean Cissell, born 13 Mar 1939 and died 6 Nov 2005 in Olympia, WA.

Claud Cissell, Vera Cissell, Ernest Cissell, and
Clarence Cissell (Beacock)

3. Claud [111]Richard "Ole" Cissell, son of Leon Albert Cissell and Clara May Thorsness was born 5 Dec 1898, in Oldham, SD. He was about 2 when his uncle Frank and aunt Cora left for Ponoka and 4 when his grandparents left.   Accordingly, he would have had few memories of their farming efforts in South Dakota. He was about 7 when his family moved from Oldham to Ponoka, and so grew up on the family farms there. Although some farm animals were still being used, tractors and other machinery were then taking over. Working on them and doing other farm work was obviously hard, but it seems to have prepared him for earning a living as an adult[112].

The 2 June 1916 Alberta census shows him still living with his grandmother and his brothers Albert and Harry on the farm near Ponoka. But by 1920 he had returned to the US and was living as one of several lodgers, and most likely farm hands, with the Sam and Elsie Patterson, stock and farming, family in Toppenish, WA [113].

---

[111] He also used the spelling of "Claude", but in later life claimed that it should have been "Claud" and so that spelling is used for this book. His signature was usually written as "C. R. Cissell".

[112] The author can remember him well coming home from work with his hands and coveralls still stained from the oil and grime of numerous vehicles, engines and other mechanical devices.

[113] When Claud left Canada and why he or the family chose to go to the Yakima area is not known. However, his grandmother, Alice, returned to the US on 13 Jul 1919 at Eastport, ID on a Canadian Pacific Railroad train. She travelled with her daughter Bessie and Bessie's family. Bessie's husband, Clinton Bailey had paid for the fares. The family was

On 14 Jun 1920 his grandmother, Alice, purchased a small house at 621 S. 15th Ave in Yakima from Lawrence and Grace Bartine. She paid $800 and assumed a $300 mortgage at 8% interest payable to Emma B. Tubbs. By 1922 Claud was living with her at that address. Claud's aunt, Bessie Bailey and her husband were living 2 doors down, at 617 15th Ave S. By 1923, Claud was working as a mechanic for the car dealer J. H. Weber, Inc[114].

Weber Chevrolet

Claud's brothers William, Ernest, and Albert were also living in the small house with their grandmother. Albert was working as a bookkeeper. In 1924 Claud's brothers William, Albert, Ernest, and Harry were all living with him. Albert's occupation then was a laborer, and so he must have had some employment problem from the previous year; Ernest was still a steamfitter; and Harry a student.

Alice Mary Bey Cissell died 14 July 1924 in St. Elizabeth's hospital[115], Yakima. She had sold her house to Claud just prior to her death[116]. She was buried in the Dakota Cemetery near Ponoka, as she had asked:

---

identified as Clinton (45), Bessie (34), Mina (15) Ada (11), Elsie (6) and Alice Cissell (69). Their race was given as "French" and their destination as Yakima.

[114] J. H. Weber began business in Yakima on 20 Sep 1922, so Claud may have been one of the company's first employees.

[115] She had been in the hospital for 60 days, from 15 May through 14 Jul 1924. The total cost for her nursing care amounted to $161.50; Claud Cissell paid most of this.

[116] On 10 Jul 1924 for $1000 from Claud and with his assumption of a mortgage to Norman Woodhouse that was for $300 at 8% interest. Albert Cissell witnessed the sale.

 In 1927 Claud's brothers Harry and Albert were still living with him. Albert was then working again as a bookkeeper and Harry as a warehouseman. William had moved to Ellensburg where he found work with a local contractor, George V. Jones.

Around Dec 1929, the house at 621 15th Ave caught fire and suffered significant damage[117]. The brothers had to find other living quarters. For several months, Claud rented room #303 at the Tieton Hotel. As indicated by the 1930 census, Harry had moved in as a lodger at the home of James W. Turner[118] and his wife Lena. By 1931 Harry had switched to the construction trade and was working as a latherer (i.e. a plasterer).

What was done day-to-day during the depression is not known. However a hint is provided by a series of checks written by Claud from 14 Feb 1930 to 10 Oct 1930 and which have survived. The total of the checks was $3010.71. If this spending rate continued for the full year it would have amounted to about $4618; probably not too bad for this time period. His expenditures indicate a continuing concern for the family. A total of about $1513 (50.3%) was given to various family members. Ernest received about $1027 (34%); Albert $210 (7%); and Vera about $125 (4%). He

---

[117] As indicated in two family letters, a young woman identified as "Pete" had gone to Seattle sometime earlier to try to get her life together and Claud had been trying to help her. One of her only two loves was her sewing machine and it had been burned up in the fire. It appears that Claud purchased a replacement White sewing machine for her in Apr 1930. Pete's other true love was "Burl" or, in her slang, "Fersin" (taken to be Montie Burl McPherson, later of Selah).

[118] May Turner, James' mother, born about 1878 in VA, was a widow in Yakima in 1920, but later married Zachariah Hawkins. Some of Claud's records that he retained from the later 1920's and 1930's include letters, photos, cards, and documents from May; from two of her other children Ruby Mae Turner (1908, WY) and Opal Chloe Turner (1909, WY); and from James' wife Lena. May's cards were usually signed as "Mother Turner" or just "Mother". It seems, then, that she had included Claud, and to a lesser extent his brothers, as part of her extended family. The reason for this family friendship is not currently known. Ruby died 29 Jun 1982 in Escondido, CA as "Ruby May Hudson" and Opal 5 Aug 1998 in Beaverton, OR as "Chloe Opal Ardinger".

spent $70 for a 1925 Chevrolet; $150 for 500 shares in a gold company; and gave $100 to Lois Holden, his girl friend. Other more mundane expenses included:

> Gas and Auto -$210
> Furniture - $148, probably to replace what had been lost in the fire.
> Insurance - $89
> Hotel - $42
> Laundry - $15
> Taxes - $22

The Apr 1930 census shows Claud living with his brother, Ernest and his family, at 134 N. 16th Ave., Yakima, WA. He was still working as an auto mechanic at Weber Chevrolet.

A photo of Claud and his co-workers in the 1920's and when he was still just a grunt:

From left to right: Oscar Newton Waltz; Clyde Bruner; Robert O. Wilson; Clinton B. Stott; Russell O. Manhart; Fred F. Hagberg; Claud Cissell; and R. Burgoz

A Photo of Claud and his co-workers in the 1930's; he was now a foreman:

From left to right: Harry T. McDaniels; Claud Cissell; Pete J. Schmalz; Edward G. Doyle; Virgil Wilson; Russell O. Manhart; Oscar Newton Waltz; Raman Berghoff; Robert O. Wilson; and William O. Brathoved (or Brathoode)

Claud met Lois Pearl Holden while working at the J. H. Weber car dealership; she worked in the office there. Family documents show they were going together before 1929 and so probably met about the time she started working at Weber's. Family tradition was that they finally decided that if they did not marry each other, neither was ever likely to find someone else to marry. Actually, though, Lois had proposed a long engagement in the early 1930's and that was what resulted.

About June 1935, Claud loaned Lois his Chevrolet so she could drive with her sister, Helen, to Enfield, IL and visit their mother's family. Lois especially liked her uncle, Willard Brockett. Nebraska and other areas had had some flooding and so she had to have the car towed across some of the rivers on the way home via Denver.

Claud and Lois with his 1931 Chevy

They were married 13 Jan 1940 in Yakima on Lois's birthday.

Lois was the daughter of William Victor Holden and Mary L. "Mollie" Brockett. (See Chapter 10 for a history of the Holden Family.) Lois had been born 13 Jan 1909 in Yakima.

Lois, High School Photo

Prior to their marriage, Claud built a house for them at 3414 Taylor Way[119] in Yakima. Construction started 5 Dec 1938. The initial cost was $9,250. On 2 Aug 1939 Claud sold the house at 621 15th Ave. S. to Walter L. Click, probably to help pay for some of the construction costs for Taylor Way.

As a couple, they enjoyed hiking and skiing. In those days ski facilities were not well developed and they generally had to carry their skis, hike up the hill, and then ski down. Lois enjoyed most sports; one Yakima newspaper article that she saved from before her marriage was titled "Chevrolet Force Picnics" and related:

> "Though she lacked the opportunities for practice that some of her married competitors could have had, Miss Lois Holden won the rolling pin throwing contest at the Weber-Buchanan Chevrolet Co. annual picnic at Eschbach's park yesterday. The one hundred persons who attended played kittyball [120], participated in races and rode horses under the direction of Malcolm Mays. Winners in some of the contests are: 50-yard dash, Mrs. Dick Reed; egg relay, Mesdames George McPeak and James Johnson; potato race, Mrs. Vern McMillan. Miss Lucille Weber starred as pitcher for the girls' kittyball team. Dinner was served at 2, and there was dancing in the evening."

By World War II, Claud was too old to serve in the military, but did want to help with the war effort. In early Aug 1942 he left Lois in Yakima and moved to the Tacoma area to work at the Mt. Rainier Ordnance Depot (MROD), Automotive Repair Division, near Tillicum. The depot repaired and refurbished military vehicles and equipment for the Army. He initially lived about 3/4 of a mile from the base, apparently in Government housing. He had a cot that would, "just fit either way" into his tiny room.

Lois continued working at Weber Chevrolet until October. She had planned to look for a job at Fort Lewis or in the local area and so rejoin with Claud. It eventually turned out that she was able to find an office job at MROD [121]. Her last day at Weber's was Saturday, 3 Oct 1942. A number of other people had left Weber's as well for the War efforts and this was causing the company difficulty in retaining employees. In one of Lois's

---

[119] [46.598369,-120.556193]

[120] Softball. The establishment of the American Softball Association in 1934 standardized the rules and name of the game that had also been known as "kitty ball", "mush ball", or "indoor baseball". See "Sports in the Western World, Revised Edition", William J. Baker, 1988, page 238.

[121] In 1943, according to their Tax Return, Claud earned $4084.15 at MROD and Lois $1937. {In 1944, Claud earned $4200.34}.

letters to Claud, she commented, "Mr. Weber surely does feel blue about everything- I really do feel so sorry for him- I told him he should put out a little sign "Closed for the duration". He said he guess(ed) he would have to do that".

After leaving Weber's she took a two or three week road trip with her sister Helen down to California to visit their youngest sister, Ruth. Helen never learned to drive, so Lois did all the driving. Cars were not very reliable at that time, but she handled the various problems (broken wind screen, carburetor repairs, failed battery cable, etc.) well.

Lois worked at MROD until 18 Mar 1944; she left claiming ill health. It is not known what the health problem was, but the couple had been having difficulty in trying to start a family.

By 1945 Claud was working as a "Dyno[122] Room Foreman". Some of the earlier officers in charge of his division, prior to May 1943, are shown on the next page.

---

[122] A dynamometer (or "dyno" for short) was used for measuring the power or torque of the engines being repaired.

1st Lt. James O. Myers[123] (Asst. Shop Sup.), 1st Lt. Warren L. Moore (Tire Reclamation), Capt. P. Laraneta[124], Edward Hudisson, Andy _____, George Yates, and 1st Lt. Albert G. Hagan (Shop Sup.)

---

[123] In Sep 1943, Lois Cissell was working as the "Control & Records" office for Lt. Myers who was then Head of the Planning & Control Department.

[124] Family records include a 1 May 1943 Western Union telegram "thank you" message to Lois at MROD from Capt P. Laraneta after he had left and was, presumably, on his way to an assignment in Europe.

The group Claud worked with at MROD included the following:

Back row (L to R): L.L. Lamoureux, L.R. Rawlings, J.A. McLaughlin, Helen Hansen, Carmen Thorpe, C.R. Cissell, Levern Rose, Dorothy McCraney, Millard(Mel) O. Leftwich, and W.D. Keffler. Front row (L to R): Thomas R. Metrician, C.E. Nelson, O.F. Johnson, R.E. Devine, and C.E. Woodward.

The couple lived in a newly constructed (1942) apartment in Tillicum on Spruce St., about 200 feet NW of the intersection with Washington Ave.[125] Their address at that time was Box 15, #3 Spruce[126]. The landlords treated them well[127].

After the war, in late Jun 1946[128], they returned to Yakima and the Taylor Way home.[129] Claud then worked as a shop foreman at the Inland Motor Company for several years.

---

[125] [47.12763, -122.547957]

[126] They were in apartment #3.

[127] The landlords were A.D. and Gertrude West.

[128] Claud's last day at MROD was 23 June 1946.

[129] "Cissell, C. R." is listed on the 1946 Roster of the Knights of Pythias, Yakima Lodge No. 53, but still with a Box 15, Tillicum, Wash. address.

About 1947/8 they also rented and started working a small truck farm in the Yakima Valley near Wapato raising large Hubbard squash for sale to Safeway, other small crops like tomatoes, and some livestock. The current address of the farmhouse is 2870 Progressive Road, Wapato[130] between Ashue Road and Higgins Lane. Claud continued at Inland Motors; working the farm in his spare time.

The author can remember one extremely hot summer day at the farm. His dad took him for a ride to the local gas station in the farm's dilapidated pickup truck. The truck was quite old, probably a Chevrolet from the 1920's or 1930's, and the floorboards were so worn that the road surface was clearly visible through holes in them. The windows were down, but provided no real cooling with the hot air blowing in. The family never spend much on non-essentials. It was an unexpected surprise, then, when Claud went to an old style Coke machine, on the left just inside a shop door. The machine had a cooling water bath and a metal track for the Coke bottles. He bought one, handed it over, and then went about his business in the shop. Probably because of the heat, and maybe because of the surprise, this was the best tasting Coke the author ever enjoyed.

The farm income was not large (about $1467 from the produce and $125 from milk and cream in the last year).

On 25 May 1950 they purchased a nearby farm[131] currently located at 2620 Progressive Road[132] from E.T. and Hazel Browning. For this they took a mortgage for $7,600 from the Prudential Insurance Company and one for $2,000 from the Brownings. The Browning loan was paid off on 29 Oct 1951.

They did not stay on the farm though. In 1950/51 they returned to Tillicum and Claud took a job back at the Mt. Rainier Ordnance Depot. They lived first nearby in a rented ranch house in American Lake Gardens, a little SW of the current Emerson Lake, and actually maintained a milk cow and a milk machine in a small adjacent barn. Lois eventually also got a job at the Ordnance Depot, working in the personnel office.

One of Lois and Claud's friends in Tillicum during the war had been "Marti" and Evelyn Frasl. Marti was a builder, and in 1951 they contracted with

---

[130] [46.419029,-120.458093]
[131] The West 1/2 of the NE 1/4 of the NW 1/4 of Section 28, Township 11 North, Range 19 East of the Willamette Meridian.
[132] [46.419029,-120.45287]

him [133] to build a home for them in Tillicum (now Lakewood, WA). Marti would later add a small extension to the SE corner of the house as a bedroom for their two older sons.

The next-door neighbors at the new house were Frank and Lois Morton Madden. Lois's first husband, Kenneth C. Codill, had been killed 13 Feb 1951 in the Korean War[134].

At the Tillicum home, Claud screened out gravel from the thin soil and used the soil for a lawn and to start and maintain a vegetable garden in the back yard. On the south edge of the garden there were a few gooseberry plants, next to the Madden's fence, that produced sour tasting fruit, but which made very good pies. A clothesline was also located in the back, nearer the house, and was used for some time even after electric dryers became more available.

Chickens were raised in a chicken-wire coop on the north side of the house for a few years. One of them, "Henny Penny", was injured when the kids accidently dropped part of the wire fence on her head as she tried to crawl under it; as a result her left eye remained useless the rest of her short life. A few pet rabbits were also raised.

Claud used the garage and driveway to work on the family car. Family cars were usually given the name, "Betsy"[135].

In the mid-1950's both continued to work at MROD. They hired Barbara Schoeppenthau part-time to care for the children. Barbara and her husband, Karl, had come to the States from Germany in 1950 and initially settled with a relative of Karl's in Centralia. Karl had been in the German Air Force during WWII, but by the 1950's was working for the Washington State National Guard at nearby Camp Murray. The Guard provided him with a private house on the base and the kids spend most summer vacation days there playing in the woods and in Murray Creek.

---

[133] The author went to school with Marti's son, Jack, and it was from him that he first learned of a baseball player named "Babe Ruth". Marti's wife, Evelyn, acted as den mother for the local Cub Scout troop. (Evelyn died in 1985, Marti in 1992, and Jack in 2009.)

[134] Lois and Ken's daughter, Nancy Marilyn, married Philip Alan Sanders in 1971, and lived in Edmonds, WA. Lois was a teacher and died 29 Apr 2007.

[135] The phrase, "Come on Betsy" was often used to encourage the vehicles to start. Other words were used when they did not.

Barbara Schoeppenthau and Lois Cissell with the children, Victor, Stephen, and David.

They paid off the mortgage on the Wapato farm on 13 Oct 1955. Then on 6 Dec 1955 they completed a real estate contract to sell it to Ivan D. and Ina Canaday; a final warranty deed for the property sale was signed by Claud and Lois on 16 Jan 1965, presumably after the Canadays had made all their required payments.

Also in the mid-1950's a fire station was built next door. One of the firemen, Bob Schultz, established a friendship with Claud and Lois. Many afternoons, after work, they would sit around the dinning room table, having a drink and discussing the weather and other local events. Bob's sister was Ellen Olsen; she owned and operated the Olsen Realty Company in Tillicum. The fireman's job gave Bob a fair number of days off between duty shifts. On those days he worked as a handyman and maintenance worker for the many rental properties that his sister managed. About 1960, he and Ellen made Claud and Lois aware of the availability of a house on American Lake and encouraged them to purchase it.

Bob also tried to help the kids come up with ways to earn some spending money. Early on, for example, he set David up with a shoeshine kit so that he could polish firemen's boots at the Station[136]. With some of their earnings, he helped them buy a new red go-cart that was used for a number of years on a track at the rear of the Station. As they got older, he showed them how to paint houses and do maintenance work and then got jobs for them during the summer with Olsen Realty. Victor expanded this to essentially a full time job for Olsen Realty during the summers in his college years and it helped pay for his college expenses.

Bob was best known for one of his euphemisms, "boy-sys". He would use it frequently in sentences such as, "Boy-sys, that was a tough job, wasn't it?"

In 1961 Claud and Lois did purchase the house on American Lake from the George Mriglot family[137]. It soon became known as the "Lake House". The house had been built in 1932 as a vacation cabin on the lake. The Mriglot's had had the house raised and placed on a cinder block foundation to create a lower floor, or above ground basement. Unfortunately, the Mriglots were somewhat short and so head clearance in the "basement" left something to be desired and was a constant nuisance.

The Lake House, itself, provided home improvement training experience for Victor and David, in part because of the amazingly (or foolishly) trusting nature of their parents. For example, the house still had the old fashioned "Wire and Knob" wiring from the 1930's. Over several years the two sons rewired the house with more modern wiring and fixtures with few major problems. There were a few problems, of course. The worst was probably the first light switch that was installed. It was made by GE and came with a 50-year warrantee. Unfortunately, not yet being

---

[136] One year Bob ran for State Insurance Commissioner; he did very poorly in the election, but the kids had fun stapling many of his campaign signs together.
[137] Total cost was $18,417.20.

knowledgeable about electrical wiring circuits, they installed it directly between the hot lead and the ground wire. This resulted in sparks, total melting of the switch, and blowing of fuses in the fuse box; but it did provide excellent training. The interior walls and ceilings were generally constructed of 1/4 inch plywood. Over time, they were replaced with more standard sheetrock material; and with only a few complains about all the dust that was created.

In 1961 the Department of Defense decided to move most of the maintenance facilities from Mt. Rainier Ordnance Depot to Toole Depot, UT. Not wanting to follow the jobs to Utah, Claud chose to retire in 1963. Lois, though, found work with the personnel office at the near-by McChord Air Force Base, and continued to work there until her retirement.

Claud died[138] on 14 Oct 1965, and Lois on 6 Sep 1982. They are buried together at Mountain View Cemetery, Lakewood, WA.[139]

As indicated above, Claud and Lois had three children:

> 3-1. David Claud Cissell, born 27 Feb 1945 in Tacoma, WA. (Continued.)
>
> 3-2. Victor Lee Cissell, born 25 Oct 1946 in Yakima, WA. (Continued.)
>
> 3-3. Stephen Holden Cissell, born 8 Sep 1951 in Tacoma, WA. (Continued.)

---

[138] In his later years, Claud suffered with heart problems and especially emphysema; possibly caused by the Camel cigarettes he had smoked much of his life. Medical tests showed that he also had had TB and which probably contributed to his problems.
[139] [47.183093,-122.493596]

3-1. David Claud Cissell, son of Claud Cissell and Lois Holden, was born at Tacoma General Hospital in Tacoma, WA on 27 Feb 1945[140]. He spent his first year in Tillicum and then went with his parents to Yakima[141] and then Wapato. After returning to Tillicum, he attended Tillicum Elementary School, Clover Park's Navy Base Middle School, Hudtloff Jr. High School, and in 1963 graduated from Clover Park High School, Lakewood, WA.

He earned a B.S. degree in Physics from the University of Washington, Seattle in 1967 and a Masters degree in Physics (experimental nuclear) from Washington State University (WSU)[142], Pullman in 1969.

He went to Air Force Basic Training in Sep 1969 at Lackland AFB TX. Attended Officer Training School (OTS) there from 20 Nov 1969 to 16 Feb 1970 as part of OTS Class 70-09, Group I, Squadron III, Flight 17 and was commissioned as a second Lieutenant. Served as a weapons (aircraft) controller, and radar countermeasures officer at McChord AFB from 1970 to 1972. Final assignment was as a Captain and as the Operations Officer for the Cape Lisburne Air Force Station on the shore of the Arctic Ocean in Alaska. He left the Air Force in Nov 1973.

After the Air Force he worked as an engineer with the Weapons Quality Engineering Center at the Naval Station at Keyport WA from Apr 1974 to Jul 1986[143]. He developed and conducted in-water reliability test programs for the Navy's CAPTOR mine system including surface- and air-

---

[140] With one minor exception, this is the birth date on all official records. One of David's cousins, Michael Allen, had been born on 26 Feb and Lois wanted her child to have the same birthday. She had discussed this with her doctor while in the hospital. She later told the author that although the doctor had told her he could not record a date different that the actual one, he had actually done just that. The official Washington State Birth Certificate states the date of birth as 2-27-45. At the bottom of the Certificate, however, is a statement from the attending physician, David H. Johnson, stating that the child was born at the hour of 12:19am on 2-26-45. From this the author concludes that he may have been born before he was born and really should have been celebrating two birthdays each year! To clarify this somewhat, Lois did record the birth on David's baby calendar as 27 Feb 1945 with the comment, "Born 12:19am 7-11ozs". So, although there is a small possibility that David might have been born very late on the night of 26 Feb, the official 27 Feb date is probably correct and will be used for this book.

[141] His mother recorded his first two questions as: 1) Who made the sky? and 2) How did the dark get into the tunnel?

[142] A family named endowment, "*The David Cissell and Julie Zalikowski Science Fund*", was established at WSU in 2014. {If you are reading this after 2114, please verify that the fund is being properly managed. Thanks. D.C.}

[143] He met his wife, Julie Ann Zalikowski, at this facility where she was a chemist in the analytical and failure analysis laboratory.

launch tests at the Nanoose underwater test range off the north east coast of Vancouver Island in Canada.

In 1975 he purchased a waterfront lot near Poulsbo. Working mostly on weekends and with tools and supplies carried in a blue Datsun 210 hatchback, he built a small cabin on the property.

David and Julie Ann Zalikowski were married on 17 Oct 1980 in Golden, CO.

Julie Ann Zalikowski, the daughter of Stanley Donald Zalikowski and Bernice Jean Zolitor, was born 11 July 1953 in Aurora, CO. She spent her entire childhood in Colorado. She attended Holy Cross Catholic School; grades 1 through 8. After leaving grade school, Julie attended Marycrest Catholic High School in Denver.

Julie earned a B.A. degree in Chemistry from University of Northern Colorado (UNC), Greely in 1975. While attending UNC she discovered the world of research, joining Dr. Roger Kovar's group as an undergraduate research scientist. It was her involvement with this group that sparked her interest in analytical instrumentation and synthetic chemistry. Upon graduating from UNC, Julie attended graduate school at the University of Washington in Seattle, WA, earning an M.S. degree in Organic Chemistry in 1979.

Her first job as a chemist was at the Keyport Navy facility in 1979 and where she did meet David[144].

In 1980 she took a job with the Department of Energy at the Rocky Flats facility, near Denver CO[145]. In 1981 she returned to the Poulsbo area; started and operated an analytical test laboratory: Pacific Analytical Laboratory Services (PALS). The success of the laboratory was, she claimed, in large part due to the help and free labor of her husband and parents. During this time Julie also worked for the Navy at the Bangor Trident Submarine Refit Facility; in their analytical laboratory.

---

[144] Julie, kindly, had a comment about this time, "During grade school at Holy Cross Catholic School, the Sisters of Charity raised concerns with my parents that I did not have a "best" friend. While I was involved in several youthful pranks in High School at Marycrest, I still left there without a real "best" friend. In this regard, I personally laid to rest all the concerns of nuns and parents after finding David."

[145] Publications while at Rocky Flats DOE Facility included: Zalikowski JA. Characterization of Hydrocarbon Distillates. Analytical Laboratory Progress Report. Rocky Flats Plant. Rockwell International, 1981.

From Jul 1986 through November 1990 David worked as manager of the Engineering Support Office at the Office of Naval Research facility in Pasadena, CA. and on the California Institute of Technology campus. He provided quality assurance coverage for Government hardware contracts with Universities in the Western United States. This effort was mainly for spacecraft instruments being built for NASA [146]. During most of this period David and Julie lived in Duarte, CA. Julie worked as an analytical chemist with the Montgomery Watson Company (MW) in Pasadena. She began her career at MW by developing test methods and supporting the company's environmental ground water evaluation and remediation projects for the EPA and other agencies[147]. Her role at MW gradually increased to include management of both the organic and inorganic analytical laboratories[148]. Her final role prior to departing MW for the east coast was as the Director of Research and Development.

From Nov 1990 through retirement in Sep 2006, David worked at NASA's Goddard Space Flight Center, Greenbelt MD. He was a quality assurance engineer and quality manager for a number of NASA space missions [149] and also supported launches at the Kennedy Space Center and Cape Canaveral Air Force Station, FL. He provided quality coverage for the first Hubble Space Telescope (HST) servicing mission, STS-61[150] that launched in Dec 1993. This mission corrected problems with the telescope's mirror. He

---

[146] These included the Faint Object Spectrograph (FOS) instrument build by UC San Diego for the Hubble Space Telescope (HST); Stanford's Total Absorption Shower Counter (TASC) for the Compton Gamma Ray Observatory; Solar/Stellar Irradiance Comparison Experiment (SOLSTICE) instrument at University of Colorado for the UARS spacecraft; Far Ultraviolet Space Telescope (FAUST) at UC Berkeley for a shuttle bay mission; several instruments at UC Berkeley, UCLA and UCSD for the WIND and POLAR spacecraft; and early NICMOS instrument efforts at the University of Arizona for HST.

[147] Publications while at Montgomery Watson included: Clark RR and Zalikowski JA. Comparison of Capillary and Packed Column Techniques for GCMS Analysis of Volatile Organic Compounds. Water quality Technology Conference, June 1987. Zalikowski JA, Wilczak A, Oelker GL. Cyanogen Chloride Determination and Formation in Drinking Water. Spectroscopy, October 1991.

[148] Main instruments included GC, GC-MS, AA and ICP.

[149] Successful projects included the Multi-mission Modular Spacecraft (MMS); Upper Atmosphere Research Satellite (UARS); Extreme Ultraviolet Explorer (EUVE); Far Ultraviolet Spectroscopic Explorer (FUSE); CLOUDSAT; Gravity Recovery and Climate Experiment (GRACE); and the Advanced Composition Explorer (ACE) (ACE was sent to the L1 Libration point, located about 1 million miles from the Earth, towards the Sun and where the Sun and Earth's gravitational fields generally cancel one another.) One interesting, but unsuccessful, mission; Vegetation Canopy Lidar (VCL) was also worked on.

[150] "STS" was a NASA acronym for "space transportation system", better known as the Space Shuttle. The number was assigned to identify the specific launch or mission being flown.

was similarly involved with the subsequent HST servicing missions 2-(STS-82, Feb 1997), 3A-(STS-103, Dec 1999), 3B-(STS-109, Mar 2002), and a major portion of the final mission 4-(STS-125, May 2009) [151].

HST 1st Servicing Mission Team[152]

David Cissell (Front row, 4th man from right). The Project Manager, "Cepi", is in a suit just to the left of the 7 astronauts sitting near the center of the photo[153].

During this time David and Julie lived on Chesapeake Bay, near Annapolis, MD which was not too far from the original Cissell family holdings in St.

---

[151] Following loss of the Space Shuttle, Columbia during reentry, in Feb 2003, NASA decided that flying a Shuttle for the 4th servicing mission would be too risky for the astronauts. David worked with the GSFC HST team in their development of the Hubble Robotic Servicing and De-orbit Mission (HRSDM) system to allow the mission to be performed on-orbit robotically. This effort was conceived and run by one of NASA's better project managers, Frank Cepollina "Cepi" and showed that almost nothing is really impossible. However, prior to construction of the flight hardware, the NASA Administrator, on 29 Apr 2005, re-authorized use of the shuttle for the 4th mission. Safety concerns were addressed, somewhat, by having a second shuttle on the launch pad during the servicing mission as a backup rescue option. Accordingly, the 4th mission was flown on the Space Shuttle and the astronauts conducted the on-orbit operations in the same way as the other missions.

[152] During the year prior to launch, this team worked at least 13 hour days, seven days a week with essentially no leaves or holidays. Following completion of the on-orbit operations, preparations for the next, more complex, mission began in about the same manner.

[153] It is noted that this work team was larger that those shown earlier for Leon and for Claud Cissell, but the work was somewhat more complicated.

Mary's County to the south. Dave even acquired a few tobacco plants from a farm in that County and grew them as the family might originally have done[154].

Julie worked first with the Lockheed Martin Corporation in Annapolis as part of their contract to operate the EPA Region III laboratory. She managed both the data management/review operations as well as the entire on-site analytical laboratory. In 1992 she took a job with the contract research pharmaceutical company, PharmaKinetics Laboratories, at 302 W Fayette St. [155] in Baltimore. There she managed the efforts of the Bioanalytical Research laboratory and once again become the Director of Research and Development.

In 1998 she accepted a position as Principle Scientist with AstraZeneca (AZ) Pharmaceuticals in Wilmington, DE. There she continued analytical chemistry efforts and managed the Wilmington bioanalytical mass spectrometer resources. She worked on the development of new drugs and was part of the team that developed the successful statin drug; Crestor.[156] [157] While with AZ, part of Julie's responsibilities required travel to other AZ sites in both England and Sweden. David was able to enjoy exploring these countries in some detail by tagging along.

---

[154] While the plants grew very well, plans to dry the leaves in an upstairs bedroom and then convert them to useful cigars did not work out as well.

[155] Just down the block from the gravesite of the writer, Edgar Allan Poe.

[156] Publications while at AstraZeneca included: Zalikowski JA, Adedoyin A, DiOrio MC. Development and Validation of a Single Bioanalytical Method for Multiple Cytochrome P450 Probe Drug Substrates. AAPS Annual Conference, Oct 2001, Denver. Zalikowski JA Automated Liquid-Liquid Extraction; Evaluation of a Commerical 96-well Format System. AstraZeneca Bioanalysis 2002 Conference, August 2002, Alderley Park, UK. Haung L, Zalikowski JA, Dudley A, Grimm S, Wang Y, Investigation of P-glycoprotein-mediated transport of Rosuvastatin Acid and its Lactone across MDR1-MDCK Cell Monolayers. Annual AAPS Conference, 2003, Salt Lake City, Utah, USA. Zalikowski JA, Ensuring Data Integrity. Cambridge Health Institute Symposium, GLP Bioanalysis: Building a Laboratory from Inside Out. 2004, Baltimore, MD,USA. Schneck D, Birmingham B, Zalikowski J, Mitchell P, Wang Y, Martin PD, Lasseter K, Brown CDA and Raza A, The Effect of Gemfibrozil on the Pharmacokinetics of Rosuvastatin. Clin Phamacol Ther. 2004; 75(5):455-463. Lee E, Ryan S, Birmingham B, Zalikowski J, March R, Ambrose H, Moore R, Lee C, Chen Y and Schneck D, Rosuvastatin pharmacokinetics and pharmacogenetics in white and Asian subjects residing in the same environment. Clin Phamacol Ther. 2005 Oct; 78(4):330-341. Lee E, Birmingham B, Zalikowski J, March R, Ambrose H, Moore R, Lee C, Chen Y, Schneck D, Rosuvastatin pharmacokinetics and pharmacogenetics in white and Asian subjects residing in the same environment. Clin Phramacol Ther. 2005; 78(4):330-341.

[157] She also taught pipetting techniques to the author to help him learn about DNA techniques for his genealogy efforts.

In 2000 Julie spent 3 months in Cairo, Egypt as part of a MW team to help set up a laboratory and train its workers at the city's water treatment facility that MW had designed and built. A number of stories resulted from this effort. One dealt with the bacteriology section of the laboratory. The team had great difficulty getting one of the technicians to consistently clean and sterilize the work surfaces. He finally explained, that he was a good Muslim, wanted to have a large family, and so didn't want to sterilize himself by using the chlorine bleach on the bench top.

Because of David's decision to retire, Julie returned to the Seattle area in 2005. She worked at Novartis Diagnostics (Chiron Corporation) in 2005 and 2006 before taking a position as Senior Scientist with the Seattle facility of Amgen, Inc. With the "outsourcing" of the Amgen work she moved in 2012 to Accium BioSciences, located in Swedish Hospital's Cherry Hill facility. Here again she managed the efforts of the Bioanalytical Laboratory and provided project management for all of the company's pharmaceutical contracts.

David returned to Washington State in Oct 2006 after the house in Annapolis had been sold. The cabin near Poulsbo was replaced with a larger home.

Julie and David at Desert Hot Springs, CA.[158]

---

[158] Staged photo in that Julie did not normally drink alcohol.

3-2. Victor Lee Cissell, son of Claud Cissell and Lois Holden, was born 25 Oct 1946 in Yakima, WA. He was born at St Elizabeth's Hospital, and so in the same building that his grandfather and namesake, William Victor Holden, had built.

Victor Cissell

Victor attended Tillicum Elementary School, Navy Base Junior High School, Iva Alice Mann Jr. High School and graduated from Lakes High School in 1964 as part of the first graduating class. Starting in high school, during summers and in his spare time, he operated a maintenance company working mostly for the Olson Realty Company in Tillicum. He attended Yakima Junior College for two years and then transferred to the University of Washington where he earned a B.A. degree in Business in 1968.

He was employed first by Lile Moving and Storage in Tacoma, 1969 - 1972. In 1974 he joined the Pacific North West Bell Telephone Company, where he worked for one day short of 32 years.

Victor provided the following remembrances in 2014:

> "My earliest memories were of the farm in Wapato, Washington. I remember my Dad going off in the fruit orchard in search of pheasants; David and I riding on a tractor (must have been 3 or 4 years old). I remember when a pig was lifted by its rear legs to be slaughtered, how it squealed.
>
> In 1950-1951 we moved to a house in American Lake Gardens. Shortly after, we moved to our new house, on Grant Ave. it was

surrounded by tall scotch broom. We cut many paths through these until Pierce County decided to build a fire station next door to us, destroying much of our trails. In the large oak trees, behind the fire station we built three story tree houses. We even had a pipe running from the second level to the ground. At one time Stephen thought he would go down like a fireman, and ran to grab the pipe, but missed and fell to the ground (it's hard to believe he didn't get hurt). This apparently was the start of many falls he would suffer later in life[159]. In the Fall, we would have acorn fights, I am surprised no one lost an eye. We had milk delivered by a milkman, as this was before refrigerated trucks, they kept the milk cold with ice, and occasionally we got some to eat. We had no phone service, so went across the street to the William Carty residence to get calls.

We spent summers at Camp Murray (a National Guard Facility south of Tillicum). Stephens's baby sitter lived there, so it was a great time to explore the creek (Murray Creek) that flowed into American Lake. We scavenged through the dump they had and stored our finds in an abandoned house we found. We even had 5-gallon gas cans filled with water so we could put out the fires they started after dumping valuable things. One day, however they found the house and demolished it.

In 1962 we moved to a house on American Lake. Bedrooms were assigned by seniority, thus David got the upstairs bedroom facing the lake. I got the upstairs bedroom facing the road. Stephen ended up in the middle bedroom down stairs. This was another great place to grow up as a child. We could explore Fort Lewis, Camp Murray, and all the inlets and swamps around the lake. We would go frogging at nights. In the summer we would go water skiing. Since we had a dock, we built a diving tower. As I remember it was about 20-25 feet high.

After graduating as the first class of Lakes High School, in Lakewood, I was accepted at Yakima Valley Junior College, In Yakima Washington (my GPA in High school was only 1.5). Starting college was important, as I needed to avoid the draft for the war in Vietnam. After two years, I transferred to Seattle University, in Seattle. But found after one Semester I could not afford the cost of a private college. I was ready to drop out when David told me as a transfer student with a 3.0 GPA, I could apply to the University of Washington, which I did, and was accepted. I graduated in 1968 with a general business degree. This turned out to be the hardest, most challenging time of my life.

---

[159] As an adult, Stephen took several falls from ladders while working around his home. A number of broken bones and other damage resulted.

My first job was working the claims department at Lile Mayflower Moving Co. But found there to be no security for long term employment. After 4 years, I quit and went to Clover Park Vocational School to become an installer for the phone company. I was hired as a service rep in 1974, by Pacific North West Bell. After 2 years, I transferred to Olympia as a cable splicer. I spent many weeks on out of town assignments, which I loved as the company paid for lodging, and all the food I ate. After 8 years in Olympia I transferred back to Tacoma. There, after 32 years (one day short), I retired.

We now travel south to California or Arizona in our 5th wheel, for 5-6 months of play each year. We have learned to play Pickleball, water volley ball and other social activities."

Victor married Judith "Judy" Emalyne Swenson (born18 Aug 1948) on 11 Apr 1981 at their home in Puyallup, WA. Judy was the daughter of Walter H. Swenson and Ellen Josephine Wales. Judy's daughter, Amy Ellen Carlson, had been born 1 Oct 1975[160]. Victor and Judy had one son, Chad Holden Cissell, born 12 Dec 1983.

3-2-1. Amy Ellen Carlson Cissell attended Western Washington University and the University of Washington and obtained education (teaching) degrees. Amy married Robert Dale Droessler on 30 Jun 2007. Amy and Robert's children include:

3-2-1-1. Quinten Harold Droessler, born 29 Mar 2010 in Puyallup, WA.

3-2-1-2. Emmitt Lee Droessler, born 8 Mar 2012 in Puyallup, WA.

3-2-1-3. Cora Eileen Droessler, born 8 Mar 2012 in Puyallup, WA.

---

[160] Amy Ellen Carlson was raised by Victor Cissell, as his own daughter. She assumed the Cissell name.

Robert and Amy with their children: Cora, Quinten, and Emmitt

3-2-2. Chad Holden Cissell, son of Victor Cissell and Judy Swenson Carlson, was born in Puyallup on 12 Dec 1983. He attended Ridgecrest Elementary School and Ferrucci Jr. High School in Puyallup. Chad was part of the first graduating class of Emerald Ridge High School in Puyallup in 2002. In 2006, he graduated with a B.A. degree in Law and Justice from Central Washington University. At the time of this book he was attending nursing school at Kaplan College in Las Vegas, NV.

Chad Cissell

Victor and Judy were divorced in 1995. Victor then found a partner, Judy Eagle[161], whom he had met at work. Judy Eagle, born 9 Apr 1946, had been married previously and had a daughter.

3-3. Stephen Holden Cissell, son of Claud Cissell and Lois Holden, was born 8 Sep 1951 in Tacoma, WA. He attended first grade at St. Francis Cabrini Catholic School in Lakewood. He then went to Tillicum Elementary School, Woodbrook Jr. High School, and graduated from Lakes High School in 1969. In 1973 he graduated from the University of Washington with a B.A. degree in Communications and Advertising.

On 27 Apr 1974 Stephen married Carol Louise Kinnune, (born 29 Dec 1951), daughter of William Paul Kinnune and Alene Lewis, in Everett WA. Stephen and Carol had two children:

> 3-3-1. Ashley Elizabeth Cissell was born 11 Nov 1980 in Bellevue, WA. She earned a B.A. degree in Political Science from the University of Washington in 2003.

>> 3-3-1-1. Kali Cissell, Ashley's first daughter, was born 22 Aug 2005 in Bellevue, WA.

> Ashley married Gregory Thomas Taleck on 11 Oct 2012 at Waimea, Kauai, HI. Ashley and Greg's children [162] include:

>> 3-3-1-2. Miles[163] Owen Taleck, born 27 Sep 2011 in San Francisco, CA.

>> 3-3-1-3. Sierra Madison Taleck, born 21 Sep 2013 in Bellevue, WA.

---

[161] To avoid confusion about the two "Judy's", the family would sometimes refer to them as "Judy #1" (Judy Carlson) and "Judy #2" (Judy Eagle).

[162] Kali Cissell Taleck was raised by Greg Taleck and she assumed his name.

[163] The children's first names were selected, in part, to represent prime numbers like their parents'. (e.g. the "S" in Sierra is the 19th letter of the alphabet and so corresponds to Ashley (1), Greg (7), Kali (11) and Miles (13)).

Miles, Kali, Ashley (holding Sierra), and Greg

3-3-2. Ryan Paul Cissell was born 7 Mar 1985 in Bellevue, WA. Ryan graduated from the University of Washington in 2007 with a B.A. degree in Communications. He married Eugénie Jeanne Marie Euphrasie Villeronce in Seattle on 22 Sep 2010. Eugénie, born 18 Jun 1986 in Marseille, France, was the daughter of Alain Villeronce and Marie-Pierre Barre. Eugénie graduated from the Université de la Méditerranée in Marseille with a Bachelor degree in Economics in 2007 and a Master of Finance degree in 2009. Their children include:

3-3-2-1. Léonie Marie Cissell , born 18 Aug 2014 in Bellevue, WA[164]. ☺

---

[164] Léonie Marie Cissell is the youngest family member to be included in this book. ☺

Ryan, Léonie, Eugénie, and Marie-Pierre Barre

Stephen and Carol were divorced in 1991. On 25 Apr 1992 Stephen married Kim Renna Pulliam in Las Vegas, NV, but that marriage ended with a divorce.

Stephen married Villette Teresa Nolon in 1996 on Elliot Bay in Seattle. Villette was the daughter of George Henry Nolon and Adele M. Pierro.

Stephen has resided in Bellevue, WA since 1975.

Villette Nolan and Stephen Cissell in Seattle

Part of this branch of the family is shown at a "Company meeting" in 2000:

Back row (L to R): David Cissell, Chad Cissell, Victor Cissell, Julie Zalikowski, Ryan Cissell, Villette Nolon. Front row (L to R): Amy Cissell, Ashley Cissell, Judy Eagle, and Stephen Cissell.

4. Albert Lewis "Jim" Cissell, son of Leon Albert Cissell and Clara May Thorsness, was born 21 Nov 1900 in Oldham, SD. In 1927 Albert was working as a bookkeeper and living with his brothers, Claude and Harry at 621 15th Ave S. in Yakima. He married Dollie Augusta Edith Turner who had been born 17 Aug 1909 in Hamilton County, New York to William H. and Nancy Edith Turner. In 1931, Albert and Dollie were living at 309 S. 6th in Yakima and Albert was an assistant manager with the Yakima Fruit Exchange. They had 4 children, all born in Yakima, WA:

>   4-1. James Albert Cissell was born about 1932. He died 23 Nov 2012 in Woodland Hills, CA. James married first Cody Elaine Russell in 1965 in Reno, NV. Cody had a son, Arnold, from a previous marriage. The marriage ended in divorced in Oct 1971 in Los Angeles. He married secondly, Madeline May Sellers on 15 Feb 1980 in Carson City, NV. Madeline had been born 14 Feb 1922 in Los Angeles, CA and died 19 Aug 2012 in Agoura Hills, CA. James had no children[165].

---

[165] Lori Sabol Bernet notes that this was because of a hunting accident when he was a boy.

4-2. Edith Vava Cissell[166] was born 22 Nov 1933. She married Joseph Sabol (born about 1933) in Los Angeles, CA on 8 Apr 1958. Their children included:

4-2-1. Steven J. Sabol, born 3 Jun 1958 in Los Angeles. He never married.

4-2-2. Lori Lynn Sabol, born 28 Oct 1959 in Los Angeles. Lori married Kevin A. Bernet on 8 Dec 1985 in Los Angeles. Kevin was born 1 Aug 1958 in Bulawayo, Rhodesia. Their children include:

4-2-2-1. Nicole Michelle Bernet, born 17 Jan 1988 in Los Angeles.

4-2-2-2. Bradley Steven Bernet, born 28 Mar 1990 in Los Angeles.

4-2-3. Donna Marie Sabol, born 20 Jun 1961 in Los Angeles. Donna married Timothy Richard Goldsmith on 22 Aug 1992 in Las Vegas, NV. Their children include:

4-2-3-1. Melissa Elaine Goldsmith, born 17 Feb 1993 in Los Angeles.

Vava married secondly, Donald J. David on 19 Jul 1970 in Los Angeles, CA. Donald had been born 27 Aug 1925 and died 21 Jan 1981 in Los Angeles, CA. Vava died as "Vava Edith David" on 2 Apr 2010 in Culver City, CA.

4-3. William Lee Cissell was born 12 Sep 1935. He served with both the Marines and with the Air Force where he was a TSgt. He died on 28 Mar 1974 and is buried in the Los Angeles National Cemetery[167]. He did not marry, but did have one daughter, Rebecca. Rebecca's mother was Harriet _____.

---

[166] Her family named her "Edith Vava", but she chose to be called "Vava Edith".
[167] In Section 70A, Row O, Site 46.

4-4. Norma Jean Cissell was born 29 Jun 1937 and died 3 Feb 2000 in Mesa, AZ. She is buried in Mesa, AZ. Norma married George Chavez. Their children, born in Belen, Valencia, NM, include:

4-4-1. Kimberly Chavez, born 5 Sep 1957. Married first, Kurt Kalbfleisch. Married secondly _____ Gibbons. Kimberly and Kurt had two daughters:

4-4-1-1. Heidi Kalbfleisch. Heidi married Andrew Peabody 4 Jul 2013 in Meza, AZ.

4-4-1-2. Alanna Kalbfleisch.

4-4-2. Matthew L. Chavez, born 31 Jul 1958. Matthew married Erin Christianson in Dec 1988. She had a daughter, Tabitha, from a previous relationship.

4-4-3. Douglas F. Chavez, born 28 Jan 1959. Douglas married Sandra Lee Simko about 2002. Children include:

4-4-3-1. Mark Chavez, born 11 Mar 1999.

4-4-4. Derrick Chavez, born 8 Jun 1960. Married Monica Smith in New Mexico. Children include:

4-4-4-1. Daniel Chavez, born 20 Mar 1987 in Anaheim Hills, CA. Married Carina Palomino 15 Aug 2014.

4-4-4-2. Michael Chavez, born 12 Jan 1989 in Anaheim Hills, CA. Married Candice _____. Children include:

4-4-4-2-1. Levi Chavez, born about Mar 2013 near Ft Collins, CO.

4-4-5. Brian Cissell Chavez, born 8 Jun 1967. Brian married Luzinda Lynn Estrada (born 31 Aug 1966). Brian and Luzinda had 7 children:

4-4-5-1. Zachary Chavez.

4-4-5-2. Joshua Chavez.

4-4-5-3. Jacob Chavez.

4-4-5-4. Maria Chavez.

4-4-5-5. John-Paul Chavez.

4-4-5-6. Simon Chavez.

4-4-5-7. Gabriel Chavez.

Kimbery, Douglas, Brian, Derrick, and Matthew Chavez

Albert Cissell[168] died in Seattle on 26 Apr 1945. Funeral services were held in Yakima on 28 April and he was buried at Terrace Heights Memorial Park[169] near Yakima.

Dollie then married Jalmer Olander Viger[170] on 4 Feb 1946 in Sunnyside, WA and had a son, Dennis Jalmer Viger. Jalmer had been born 30 Jul 1908 in ND to Oscar Viger and Gina Lundeby. Jalmer died 20 Jun 1956 and is buried in the Terrace Heights Cemetery. After Jalmer's death, Dollie

---

[168] Albert had suffered with TB from 1942 or earlier. He was taken to the Laurel Beach Sanatorium in Seattle on 23 April 1945 and died there three days later.

[169] Block 5, Section 76, Lot 3. [approx. 46.607735, -120.45717].

[170] Jalmer Viger is buried at the Terrace Heights Cemetery, Block 27, Section 115, Lot 5 [approx. 46.60728, -120.45736].

married, Otto Cecil White [171] in Las Vegas, NV on 13 Jun 1959. She married fourthly, Harold Miller (born 1914) on 28 Dec 1964, Yakima, WA. Dollie died in late Oct 1975 while visiting with family in Belen, NM.

5.   Harry Norman[172] Cissell, son of Leon Albert Cissell and Clara May Thorsness, was born 27 May 1907 in Ponoka, Alberta. He married Ava Marina Scott (born 13 Jul 1916 in Taney County, MO) on 15 Jun 1935 in Yakima. Ava was the daughter of James W. Scott and Laura Belle Mowrey. Harry worked as a carpenter, first in Yakima and then in the Olympia area. Harry and Ava had two children:

5-1.   Ronald Norman Cissell, born 20 Dec 1936 in Yakima, WA. Ronald married (1) Peggy Leach. She had a daughter, Susan (born 1957), from a previous marriage and whom Ron did adopt. Ronald married (2) Jenevieve M. Wanner (born 22 Sep 1938, WI) on 4 Aug 1961.   Children associated with this marriage include Shaun and Deanna. Ronald married (3) Virginia Lee (Davis) Westfall (born 27 May 1926, WV) on 11 Feb 1970 (Virginia had previously married and divorced Billy E Tyson and subsequently married Jack R. Sweetser on 8 Sep 1973 near Olympia.) Ronald married (4) Marjorie L. Lowe (born 2 Sep 1938, OR) about 16 Oct 1981.   Ronald worked for the Washington State Department of Highways, Planning Commission. Ronald died 6 Jan 1991 in Olympia[173].

5-1-1.   Belinda J., born about 1958. Ron may have been her father, but this has not been proved. Belinda married first Leroy K. Lemnah and secondly Timothy D. Conley of Evans, WA. She had at least one daughter, Tania Dawn. Tania married ___ Iverson on 2 Sep 2006 and had children.

5-1-2. Shaun Alexander Norman Cissell, born 2 Jun 1962 to Ron Cissell and Jenevieve Wanner. Shaun married Ruby Lucille Hammontree (born about 1959) on 12 Jan 1987 in Carson City, NV. He also married Christine Lea Paige (born 15 Oct 1964) on 7 Aug 1993 in Union County, OR. Shaun's children included:

---

[171] Otto White was born 14 Jan 1905 and died 29 Oct 1983. He is buried at Shoshone Cemetery, ID.

[172] It appears that Harry's middle name was taken from his Grandmother, Ulrikka's maiden name.

[173] Accurate documentation of this family is difficult. Ron's obituary in the Olympian newspaper incorrectly identifies his mother, but lists 3 daughters, Suzan Spellman of Auburn; Deanna Colley of Gainesville, FL; and Belinda Lemnah of HI.

5-1-2-1. Alexander J. Cissell, born 16 Mar 1989.

5-1-2-2. Tomas C. Cissell, born 18 Jun 1990.

5-1-3. Deanna, born 5 May 1964 to Jenevieve Wanner after her divorce from Ron. Father is believed to have been Ron.

Ronald Cissell in 1955

2. Sharon (Sharyn) Lee Cissell, born 1939 in Yakima, WA. Sharon married Larry Dewayne Maulding (born 10 Apr 1938, died Dec 1989 in WA). Sharon and Larry divorced, but had two children:

2-1. Larry Michael Maulding born 7 Aug 1957 in San Diego, CA. Larry married Alice M. Gonzalez on 3 Aug 1985 in Ventura, CA. Children included:

2-1-1. Jennifer M Maulding, born about 1987. She married Derick Walker 16 Jun 2012 at Lincoln, CA.

2-2. Jerald David Maulding, born 11 Sep 1958. Died 18 Nov 2009 in Oxnard, CA. Jerald did not marry.

Sharon married secondly, Vincent Arnold Froemel. Vincent was born 26 Aug 1934 in MN and died 22 May 2009 in Duluth, MN. He is buried in Greenwood Cemetery in Hayward, WI. They divorced in Feb 1976, but had Children:

2-3. Lori (Laura) Anne Froemel, born 9 Apr 1969, Hennepin, MN. Married Jeffery Allen Samples, 28 Jan 1994 Las Vegas, NV. Married Mark Meister about 4 Mar 2010, HI. Children:

> 2-3-1. Brookly Anne Froemel, born 8 Dec 1985, Venura, CA (Father ukn). Married Paul Anthony Rangere (born 7 Jul 1984, Ventura, CA.), Lane County, OR. (Before 2009). Married (Jeremy P.?) Lahmann. Children included:
>
> > 2-3-1-1. Deegan Joseph Lahmann, born 5 Sep 2010 in Oxnard.

2-4. Vincent Marshall Froemel, born 26 Oct 1970, Alameda, CA.

Ava Scott died 3 Apr 1939 in Yakima of pneumonia and was buried there at the Terrace Heights Cemetery[174]. Harry married secondly, Geraldine (Jeraldine) Marie Calvin on 9 November 1946 in Olympia, WA. His bother "E. L. Cissell" was one of the witnesses on the marriage certificate. Geraldine (Jera/Jeraldine) was born 24 Mar 1919, Chouteau Montana. Her parents were John F. Calvin and Blanche M. McBean. The marriage seems to have ended by 1963 as Jeraldine married Richard K. Carmoney on 1 Oct 1963 in San Mateo County, CA. This marriage also ended in divorce in Jan 1966 in San Francisco. She later married Richard R. Craig, on 5 Apr 1971 (as Jeraldin M. Calvin) in Contra Costa County, CA. She died 28 Dec 2008 in Oxnard, CA as "Jera Craig" [175].

Harry died 27 Sep 1982, Olympia, WA and is buried at Olympic Memorial Gardens, Tumwater, WA.

---

[174] Block 10, Section 17, Lot 5 [approx. 46.61009, -120.45969]. Her family provided no marker.

[175] Sharon's son, Larry Michael Maulding, cared for Jera prior to her death.

Leon Cissell

9. Yakima, Washington
Bessie Cissell

Bessie (Carrie) Cissell (1885 - 1947). Bessie Cissell, daughter of Nerius Cissell and Alice Bey, was born in Ashland Township, Dodge County [176], MN on 5 Apr 1885. She married Clinton "Mac" Dewitt Bailey on 20 Jan 1904 in Ponoka, Alberta; Emma and Emil Wold were the bridesmaid and best man. Bessie was 5'- 3" tall, with brown hair and blue eyes.

Clinton had been born Nov 1873 in New Lisbon, Juneau County, WI. His parents were Charles Oliver Bailey (born Oct 1845 in Ohio) and Minerva A. Carpenter (born Dec 1850 in WI). Charles had served with Wisconsin's 9th Regiment in the Civil War. Charles and Minerva had married in 1868. Their children included:

1. Leslie V. Bailey, born Apr 1869, WI.
2. Henry H. Bailey, born Jul 1871, WI.
3. Clinton Dewitt Bailey, Nov 1873, WI.
3. Laura M. Bailey, born Aug 1879, MN.
4. Clifford E. Bailey, born Mar 1882, SD.
5. Elmer C. Bailey, born Sep 1884, SD.
6. John E. Bailey, born Jan 1887, SD.
7. Raymond M. Bailey, born Feb 1891, SD.

By 1880, the Charles Bailey family had moved to farmland near Madison, Lake County, SD. This was about 16 miles from Oldham, where the Cissell family would later settle. In 1900 Charles and Minerva were farming in Idaho, and living in Tammany Precinct, Nez Perce County, near Lewiston. By 1915 they had retired back to Madison, SD. Charles died there in 1916 and Minerva in 1924[177]

Bessie and Clinton had 4 children all born in Ponoka, Alberta:

9-1. Minerva [178](Mina or Pauline) Bailey, born 13 Nov 1904. Minerva married John Manly Hull on 29 Dec 1921 in Yakima, WA[179]. John had

---

[176] Bessie's Obituary on page 3 of the Yakima Morning Herald for Wed 19 Feb 1947 gives her birthplace as Faribault, MN; about 30 miles NW of Ashland.

[177] They are buried in the Graceland Cemetery, Madison, SD.

[178] "Minerva", was taken from the name of Clinton Bailey's mother.

been born 5 May 1899 in Paton, Greene County, IA. John married secondly, Mary Schuler (born about 1903 in MT.). John Hull died 24 Mar 1982[180]. Minerva and John had two children before she left him and the children. Mary had had three children prior to her marriage to John. The five children raised by John were:

> 9-1-1. Glenn Arthur Hull, son of Minerva and John, born 25 Feb 1923. Glenn married an Indian woman, Elaine Helen Carl (Born 16 Feb 1924 in White Swan, WA) on 5 Jun 1941 in Yakima, WA. They divorced about 1953. He married secondly, Barbara Lou Swanson (born 15 Sep 1932) in 1985. Elaine died 17 Apr 1985[181]. Glen died 30 Aug 2010 at Toppenish, WA. Glen and Elaine had 5 children:
>
> > 9-1-1-1. Ronald William Hull. Born 8 Sep 1944 in Yakima, died 11 Nov 1975 in Odesa TX. Married ____. Children included:
> >
> > > 9-1-1-1-1. Eric Hull.
> > >
> > > 9-1-1-1-2. Clay Martin Hull, born 8 Aug 1971. Married Shannon Leann Nylander Feb 2003 in Yakima?
> > >
> > > 9-1-1-1-3 Shannon Hull?
>
> 9-1-1-2. Carl Francis Hull[182], born 8 Jul 1942 in Wapato. Died 15 Aug 2008 at Gleneden Beach, OR, while on vacation. Buried at Wenas Cemetery, Selah, WA[183]. Married Arlene Louise Mattern (born 3 Apr 1943) on 29 Sep 1962. They had one son:
>
> > 9-1-2-2-1. Brian C Hull, born 11 Feb 1966. Brian married Jennifer J. Mercy (born 10 May 1976). They had children, all born in Yakima.

---

[179] Witnesses were her mother, Bessie Bailey, and her cousin, Claud Cissell.

[180] John is buried at Reservation Community Memorial Park, Wapato. Section B, Lot 18, Plot 12 [approx. 46.448654, -120.537254].

[181] Elaine is buried at Reservation Community Memorial Park, Wapato. Section C, Lot 51, Plot 4. [46.448717,-120.538265]

[182] Carl's Indian name with the Yakima Tribe was "White Buffalo".

[183] Section A, Block 14, Plot 6 [46.448717,-120.538265].

9-1-1-3. Joyce Hull, born about 1945 in WA. Died 5 Aug 1945, Yakima, WA.

9-1-1-4. Stephen Alan Hull, born 13 Sep 1946. Stephen married Paula Josephine Dufault 29 Nov 1969 in White Swan, WA. Paula had been born 1 Nov 1946 in Yakima. Their children included:

 9-1-2-4-1. Richard Hull.

 9-1-2-4-2. Christina Hull. Married ___ Bonewell.

 9-1-2-4-3. Rebecca Hull. Married ____ Correll.

 9-1-2-4-4. Alaina M. Hull, born 15 Feb 1986.

9-1-1-5. Larry Hull. Died as an infant.

9-1-2. Lorraine A. Hull, daughter of Minerva and John, born 12 Sep 1924 in Wapato, WA. She married Lloyd "Bud" Sylling 21 Jul 1942 in Yakima, WA. Lloyd had been born 8 Mar 1922 in North Dakota. Lloyd died 16 Apr 2002 in Yakima. Lorraine died 26 Jun 2008. They had 5 children:

 9-1-2-1. Phyllis Lorraine Sylling, born Feb 1944 in Wapato. Married Michael Miller. They had a son, Timothy Michael Miller born 21 Jul 1962.

 9-1-2-2. Jean Marie Sylling, was stillborn in 1947.

 9-1-2-3. Johnny Lloyd Sylling, born Jun 1949. Died 31 Mar 2013 at Lakewood, WA. Johnny had at least 4 wives (possibly including Deborah J. Smith and Linda Mims); the last being Deanna Marie Swan who he married in Jan 2000 in Yakima. John's children included:

  9-1-2-3-1. Johnny Lloyd Sylling, Jr., born about 1970. He married Katie Ivey ___ (born about 1978) and they had two children, Grace and Warren.

  9-1-2-3-2. Stace Sylling changed his name to "Jim Cline"

9-1-2-1-3. Linda Hale, was born to a women Johnny did not marry and may have lived in CA.

9-1-2-3-4. Sarah Lee Sylling. Married Blake Ourso. They had a daughter Haylee born about Jul 2013.

9-1-2-3-5. Phillip W. Sylling, born 1 Mar 1975. Not married as of Jan 2014.

9-1-2-4. Bobbi Ray Sylling, born 27 Jun 1954 in Yakima. Married Mike A. Gillespie (born 7 Sep 1953). Children included:

9-1-2-4-1. Jason Allen Gillespie, born 15 Jun 1981. Divorced from Cara Watts. They had no children.

9-1-2-4-2. Ryan James Gillespie, born 9 Feb 1985. Married Whitney Pilz (born 2 Jul 1982) about 2012.

9-1-2-5. Rebecca "Becky" Sylling, born 27 Jun 1954 in Yakima. Married Oscar Finley. Children included:

9-1-2-5-1. Oscar Charles Jr. "Charlie" Finley, born 5 Sep 1976.

9-1-2-5-2. Brian Finley, born 5 Apr 1982.

9-1-3. Ray M. Hull, born about 1921 Son of Mary Schuler, and stepson to John. Ray married Dorothy A. ___. Their children included:

9-1-3-1. Raymond H. Hull, born 21 Jul 1944. Raymond married Marcy L. Ray (Born 28 Nov 1945). Their children included:

9-1-3-1-1. Raymond N. Hull, born 16 Nov 1966. Married ____ Nelson and had Halee & Chloe.

9-1-3-1-2. Camille Dee Hull, born 16 Nov 1966. Had children Sidney, Easton & Brynne(?).

9-1-3-1-3. Heather Annette Hull. Married __ Stewart. Had triplets: Emma, Jake & Kade. Also Lily & Paul.

9-1-4. Walter Hull. Son of John & Mary. Died before 2008.

9-1-5.   Carl Emerson Hull, born 12 Oct 1923. Son of Mary Schuler and stepson to John Hull. Married Donna Yavon ____, born 13 Jun 1927. Carl had son Terry who married Carol _____ and had children Raylynn and Travis. Travis married Paula _____ and had 3 boys & 1 girl.

9-1-6.   Carol Ann Hull. Daughter of John & Mary. Married George Baker.

After leaving John Hull and their children, Minerva married James Morris in Tacoma, WA on 2 Jan 1929. In the 1930 census for Tacoma, WA she listed her name as "Pauline A. Morris", but her husband was not present.

 As "Mina Morris" of Entiat, WA, she married thirdly, Harold E. Mitchell in Ellensburg, WA on 25 Aug 1937.   Harold Emmett Mitchell had been born in 1903 and died 3 Feb 1950 in Yakima.

The obituary for Minerva's father, Clinton Bailey in Jan 1940, lists her as "Mrs. Pauline Mitchell of Hoquiam". She can be found in the 8 Apr 1940 Census for Hoquiam, WA as "Pauline Mitchell" and married, but her husband is not listed; he is listed instead with his mother and her second family in Ellensburg.

As "Pauline Alice Mitchell" she married fourthly, Clifford Wesley Hyde on 12 Nov 1944 at Spanaway, WA[184]. Clifford died 13 Aug 1955 in Yakima, age 48 and is buried at Terrace Heights Memorial Park, Yakima.

Minerva married fifthly, _____[185]McTeer.

 Minerva died 12 Nov 1969 in Yakima as "Pauline A. McTeer" and was buried in West Hills Memorial Park[186], Yakima. John Hull died 24 Mar 1982 in Toppenish, WA and was buried 27 Mar 1982 at the Wapato Reservation Cemetery, Yakima County, WA.

---

[184] The date and location suggests that Clifford Hyde may have been a soldier at near-by Fort Lewis, but this has not been verified.

[185] Ukn, but may have been William Kenneth McTeer (6 Jul 1900 - 28 Dec 1963, MO).

[186] In Apostles Section, 43C, #4 [approx. 46.58079, -120.66544]. She has no marker.

9-2. Ada Bailey was born Dec 1908. She attended high school in Yakima where she had an interest in sports[187]. She married first Alvin E. Chamberlain on 23 May 1927 in Ellensburg, WA. Alvin was the son of Joseph Flint Chamberlain and Margaret Mowery. Alvin had been born 29 Apr 1902. He died 1 Nov 1959 and is buried at the Terrace Heights Cemetery. Ada and Alvin had 2 children:

9-2-1. Gerald Alvin Chamberlain, born 18 Apr 1928 in Yakima and died 9 Sep 1984 in Yakima. Gerald married Kathleen M. Wissink in 1949 in Coulee City, WA. Kathleen was born 17 Oct 1931. Children included:

9-2-1-1. Karen Ann Chamberlain, born 23 Jul 1950 in NY. Married first Charles La Verne Honaker (born 21 May 1947) 21 Sep 1968 in Entiat, WA. Karen married secondly, Richard Horn and Thirdly, Richard Howland. Karen and Charles had one child:

9-2-1-1-1. Kristopher Honaker, born 26 Jan 1969 in Seattle. Kristopher married Regina F. Helton. Children include:

9-2-1-1-1-1. Riley Michelle Honaker, born 24 May 1999, Spokane.

9-2-1-1-1-2. Rachel Elizabeth Honaker, born 9 Sep 2003 in Spokane.

9-2-1-1-1-3. Ryan Kristopher Honaker, born 6 Dec 2005 in Spokane.

9-2-1-2. Gayle Marie Chamberlain, born 3 Oct 1952, Santa Barbera, CA. Married Richard M. Cooper (born 29 May 1946). They had two children:

9-2-1-2-1. Shannon M. Cooper (born 5 Nov 1975), married Jerome Cruzen (born 6 Apr 1972). Children included:

---

[187] The sophomore section of the Yakima High School yearbook (Lolomi) for 1926, page 53, recorded, "Ada Bailey received a numeral for volleyball".

9-2-1-2-1-1. Flora Michelle Cruzen, born 15 Jul 2005.

9-2-1-2-1-2.   Tristen Cruzen, born 25 Nov 2006.

9-2-1-2-1. Jamie Cooper (born 16 Jun 1979).

9-2-1-3. Kelli Jean Chamberlain, born 10 Oct 1954. Kelli married Kenneth Barton, but the marriage ended in divorce.

9-2-1-4. Victoria "Tori" Jo Chamberlain, born 17 Oct 1965 in Wenatchee, WA. Married Gregg F. Bailey (born 6 Jan 1966) and had a daughter:

9-2-1-4-1. Kendall Bailey, born 24 Aug 1999.

9-2-2. Beverly Mona Chamberlain, born 13 Jul 1929 in Yakima. Beverly married first Donald Leroy Pulliam (born 15 Jul 1926, died 28 May 2012) on 2 Nov 1946 in Ellensburg[188], secondly Leroy W. Johnson (born 8 Apr 1931?) and thirdly Victor B. Sinnott in 1951. Victor had been born in Hibbing, MI about 1921. Victor died on 18 Dec 1999 and Beverly on 29 Dec 2003 in Spokane. Beverly had 5 children:

9-2-2-1. Donna Lee Pulliam Sinnott, daughter of Beverly and Donald Pulliam, was born about 1947. Donna married Edgar M. Stemen. Married 2ndly ____ Volland.

9-2-2-2. Jeroline "Jerri" Lynn Johnson Sinnott, daughter of Beverly and Leroy Johnson, born 3 Aug 1949 in Yakima. Jerri married first John Groh (born 18 Dec 1948?). She married secondly, Samuel J. Via, born 16 Apr 1948, on 18 Jan 2003 in San Diego, CA. Sam died 9 Jan 2008 in WA.

9-2-2-3. Ronald Neil Sinnott, son of Beverly and Victor Sinnott, born 9 Aug (8 Sep?)1954 in Spokane, WA. Married Janet Nadine Riegel, a widow and daughter of

---

[188] The witnesses on the marriage certificate were Beverly's aunt Elsie, identified as "Elsie Van Atta" and John Mattox (Jr?) (Elsie's next, and last husband to be).

Curtis Comstock and Yvonne Hammock (born 3 Feb 1954 in CA) on 22 Mar 2002 in Spokane.

9-2-2-4. Sharon M. Sinnott, daughter of Beverly & Victor Sinnott, born 3 Apr 1958 in Spokane. She married Terry N. Pierce. Terry had been born 11 Nov 1947. Sharon had one child:

> 9-2-2-4-1. Lindsey M. Pierce, son of Sharon Sinnott and _____ Henson [189], born 31 Aug 1986.

9-2-2-5. Baby Sinnott, son of Beverly M. and Victor Sinnott. Born and died 6 Jun 1960, Spokane.

Ada married secondly Herschel B. McNair, on 1 Apr 1946 in Yakima . Herschel had been born 28 Oct 1902 in Columbia, MS[190]. He had been married previously, but came to Washington State in 1942 to work on the Hanford Project. Herschel died 25 Feb 1973 in Entait, WA. Ada died 15 Dec 1982 in Spokane, WA. Ada and Herschel had one child:

> 9-2-3. Dennis McNair, born 1 Nov 1948 in Yakima. He had a number of wives including: Judith Marie Lawson (25 Feb 1949 - 8 Nov 2003) who he married on 7 Oct 1967 at Ephrata, WA; Diana K. Spruell (born 17 Mar 1955) who he married in Kansas City, MO. in Nov 1976[191]; Sue Kissinger; Dorothy Aldin; and Kathleen L. Russell (Kish), born 2 Aug 1951. Dennis had at least five children:

> 9-2-3-1. Shawn McNair. Son of Dennis and Judith Lawson, was born in 1967.

> 9-2-3-2. Tara McNair, daughter of Dennis and Diana. Born in 1977. Children include:

> 9-2-3-2-1. Preston Shaffer, born 10 Dec 1993.

---

[189] Sharon did not marry _____ Henson. Their daughter, Lindsey, was adopted and raised by Terry Pierce.

[190] His obituary (in the Wenatchee Daily World for 26 Feb 1973, page 7) gives a birth date of 28 Dec 1902, but the 28 October 1902 date from published Social Security records is taken to be correct.

[191] There is a record for Dennis McNair and Diana K. Spruell noted in the Kansas City Times for 23 Nov 1976, page 9.

9-2-3-2-2. Kailyn Hammer, born 29 Sep 1997.

9-2-3-3. Shane Robert McNair, son of Dennis and Diana, born 6 Aug 1979. Shane had a daughter:

9-2-3-2-1. Britany Marie McNair, born 28 Jun 1999. Her mother was Jenn Stokes.

9-2-3-4. Tawnya McNair. Daughter of Dennis and Linda McCart. Married _____ Jordon. Children included:

9-2-3-3-1. Paige Jordon.

9-2-3-3-1. Hayden Jordon.

9-2-3-3-2. Ethan Jordon.

9-2-3-5. Brent McNair[192], born about 1974. Son of Dennis McNair and Linda McCart. It is not believed that Dennis and Linda ever married. Brent was married for a short time and had one son.

9-3. Melvin Everett Bailey, born 20 May 1911. Melvin married Florence Woodard 6 Oct 1933 in Ellensburg, WA[193]. They had no children. Melvin married secondly, Annabelle Z. Zimmerman on 7 Apr 1947. Annabelle had been born 10 Jan 1922. She died 10 Sep 2009 at Battleground, WA. Melvin Bailey died 29 May 1996 in Woodland, WA. Melvin and Annabelle raised 5 children, 3 were daughters from Annabelle's first marriage:

9-3-1. Connie G. Bailey, stepdaughter, was born 1940. She married Gerald L. Tallmadge. Gerald had been born in 1941.

9-3-2. Bonnie Bailey, stepdaughter, was born 13 Jun 1941. She married John E. Bucholtz. John had been born 8 Mar 1937.

9-3-3. Donna Bailey, stepdaughter, was born about 1943. Donna died in 1981.

---

[192] Coincidentally, Brent was a high school volleyball coach in Eaton CO for a niece, Christy Gabel, of Julie Zalikowski, the author's wife.
[193] Melvin's father, Clinton Bailey, was listed as one of the witnesses on the marriage certificate.

9-3-4. Melvin Frederick Bailey, son of Melvin and Annabelle, was born in 1948. Melvin married Linda Mae Simonson on 29 Jan 1971 at Woodlawn, WA. Children included:

9-3-4-1. Darrin Everitt Bailey, born 18 May 1971. Darrin had at least one child:

9-4-4-1-1. A daughter.

9-3-4-2. Andrea Doreen Bailey, was born 23 Oct 1972. Andrea married John Glen Blanchard (born 14 Nov 1959) on 6 Jun 1992 in Woodland, WA. The marriage ended in divorce, but they had two children.

9-3-4-2-1   Michael John Blanchard, born 26 Oct 1991.

9-3-4-2-2   Taylor Blanchard, born about 1995.

9-3-4-3. Darrell L. Bailey. Born about 1976.

9-3-5. Janet K. Bailey, daughter of Melvin and Annabelle, was born 25 Mar 1951. She married Gary A Matthiesen on 16 Nov 1974 in Vancouver, WA. Gary had been born 15 Sep 1948. Janet remembers Harry Cissell visiting her parent's home to play cribbage with her father, Melvin. She also remembers Emma Cissell Olmstead coming down from Ponoka to visit them. Janet and Gary had two children:

9-3-4-1. Brad J. Matthiesen, born in 1981.

9-3-4-2. Megan Marie Matthiesen, born 14 Jul 1983 in Vancouver, WA. She married Joshua Robert Robson (born 20 Jun 1981) on 12 Oct 2006 in Vancouver, WA.

Harry Cissell, Emma Cissell Olmstead, and Melvin Bailey

9-4. Elsie (Alice[194]) Bailey was born 16 Jan 1914 and died 30 May 1981 as "Elsie Emma Mattox" near Portland OR. She married first Virgil Lloyd Garrison on 29 Aug 1932 in Seattle. They had one child:

> 9-4-1. Donald Dean Garrison, born 25 Sep 1932 in Yakima, WA. Donald married Bethine Vonita Fetters (born 1936 in NE) on 20 Dec 1953. Donald died 20 Nov 1991 in Portland. The marriage ended in divorce. Bethline married secondly Martin Fernandez Orta in Anchorage, AK (ended in divorce), thirdly Jack Lewis DeLong in Portland. After the death of Jack Lewis, she married Hershel Valentine Siron. Donald and Bethine had three children:

>> 9-4-1-1. Dale Alan Garrison, born 12 Jul 1955. Dale married first, Donna Marie Hall (born about 1956). The marriage ended in divorce. Dale Alan Garrison married secondly, Katherine (Kathi) Joanne Polizzi (born 12 May 1964) on 20 Feb 1998 in Vancouver, WA. By the first marriage, Dale and Donna had 3 children:

---

[194] The 1916 Alberta census lists her name as "Alice Bailey", age 2.

9-4-1-1-1. David Vonley Garrison, born 23 Sep 1974. David married Meadow Dorne on 1 Nov 2003 in Portland. Their children included:

> 9-4-1-1-1-1. Anthea Datura Garrison, born 23 Jan 2005.

> 9-4-1-1-1-2. Bailin Rain Garrison. He was born 20 Sep 2008.

9-4-1-1-2. Daniel James Garrison, born 24 Jan 1976. Married Abigail Marie Zarosinski (born 25 Aug 1986) on 16 Jun 2011 in Vancouver, WA. Children included:

> 9-4-1-1-2-1. Henry Dean Garrison, born 24 Jan 2013.

9-4-1-1-3. Douglas Dean Garrison, born 24 Jan 1978. Married Laura N. Bailey (born 10 Mar 1977) on 11 Oct 2008 in Tacoma, WA. Children included:

> 9-4-1-1-3-1. Declan James Garrison, born 25 Apr 2012.

> 9-4-1-1-3-2. Son, Liam Alan Garrison, born 25 July 2014.

9-4-1-2. Don Robert Garrison, born 31 May 1957. Don married first Angle Beck (born 24 Apr 1958), but they divorced. He married secondly Cheryl Lynn Webb, but they divorced. He then remarried Angel Dolphine Sadler Beck on 1 Feb 2012 in Portland, OR. Don and Cheryl raised two adopted children who were biological siblings, both born in Astoria, OR:

> 9-4-1-2-1. Emily Kate Garrison, born 28 Dec 1996.

> 9-4-1-2-2. Jordan Maximillion Garrison, born 20 Nov 1999.

9-4-1-3. Debra Lynn Garrison, born 25 Jul 1959. Debra married David Barrera (born 13 Aug 1957) on 1 Oct 1976 in Anchorage, AK. Their children included:

9-4-1-3-1. Deann Bethine Barrera.   She was born 12 Jul 1978. She married Tim Cain on 5 Oct 2002, but divorced about 1 year later.

9-4-1-3-2. Aric David Barrera, born 24 Aug 1979. Aric married Brenda Kaye Beyer(Born 22 Nov 1979) on 14 Sep 2002. Their children included:

> 9-4-1-3-2-1. Emma Lauren Barrera, born 22 Nov 2003.

> 9-4-1-3-2-2. Cole Jaxon Barrera, born 5 Jul 2005.

> 9-4-1-3-2-3. Olivia Morgan Barrera, born 4 Nov 2008.

> 9-4-1-3-2-4. Kourtney Paige Barrera, born 8 Sep 2010.

9-4-1-3-3. Jared Elias Barrera, born 9 Dec 1980. Jared married Tanya Adams (Born 12 Dec 1980) on 28 Sep 2002. Their children included:

> 9-4-1-3-3-1. Caitlin Barrera, born 16 Jul 2004.

> 9-4-1-3-3-2. Jackson Jared Barrera, born 21 May 2007.

> 9-4-1-3-3-3. Carson David Barrera, born 15 Jan 2009.

> 9-4-1-3-3-4. Aslin Barrera, born 18 Aug 2012.

9-4-1-3-4. Aaron Sixto Barrera, born 7 Feb 1983.

Elsie married secondly, James Parkison Van Atta on 2 Jun 1935 in Los Angeles (as Elsie Emma Garrison, age 24).   James had been born about 1905 in PA (Father was James P. Van Atta, mother was Etta (Margaret?) Calahan). The 1940 census shows James and Elsie as ages 34 & 26, living at 1550 West 12 Place, Los Angeles with a son Donald D. Van-Atta age 7, born in WA. (This was actually Elsie's first son, Donald Dean Garrison, born in Yakima in 1932[195]). James is identified as a butcher in a retail meat market. James died 11 Jun 1945 in Yakima, WA[196].

After James' death, Elsie married thirdly, John P. Mattox. Elsie and John had 1 child:

> 9-4-2. Scott Vaughn Mattox, born 25 Dec 1947 in Yakima. Scott married Diane Marie _____(born 1 Oct 1949, Eureka, IL). Children include:
>
>> 9-4-2-1. Anne Marie Mattox, born about 1981. Married Ian Parks. Children include:
>>
>>> 9-4-2-1-1.   Elsie Parks, born about Jan 2013, Portland.
>>
>> 9-4-2-2.   David Michael Mattox, born about 1983. Graduated from the University of Portland in 2004. David married Davina Mendiburu, 3 Jun 2010.

The 1910 US Census shows Bessie and her family living at her in-laws' home in Tammany, ID. The 1930 US Census shows her in Yakima, WA, but divorced from Clinton Bailey. In 1936, Bessie married secondly, Walter W. Davis in Yakima, WA. Walter had been born in MA about 1886. In 1940 Bessie and Walter were living at 110 S. 10th Ave., Yakima. They had no children. Bessie died 18 Feb 1947 in Yakima. She was buried 21 Feb 1947 in the Terrace Heights Memorial Park[197], near Yakima as "Bessie May Davis". Clinton DeWitt Bailey died 27 Jan 1940 in Portland, OR and is also buried at Terrace Heights Memorial Park[198].

---

[195] Donald did not learn of his biological father until he found his birth certificate while the family was packing to move back to Yakima from Los Angeles. Elsie often had her father take care of the boy.

[196] James is buried at Terrace Heights, Block 17, Section 50, Lot 3. [approx. 46.609118,-120.459241]. He has no formal marker.

[197] Block 23, Section 101, Lot 6. [approx. 46.60874, -120.45839]. Bessie has no formal marker.

[198] Block 15, Section 37, Lot 6. [approx. 46.609526,-120.460029]. He has no formal marker.

10. The Holden Family

The Holden family history in the US began with Michael Holden, born 21 Mar 1824 in South Croxton, England. He married Elizabeth Orme (21 Oct 1827) in Whitwick, Leicestershire, England on 10 Aug 1847. They became Mormons and came to the US with a group of similarly minded families intending to settle in Salt Lake City (SLC), UT. They had a daughter, Jane, who had been born at Coalville, Leicestershire 25 July 1848 (died 27 Oct 1938, SLC, UT). Many of the Mormon immigrants from England took ships to New Orleans and then boats up the Mississippi to St. Louis to reach a staging or rest site at Gravois, MO. It appears that Michael and Elizabeth probably followed this same route. They came with their daughter, Jane Holden. A second daughter, Mary Elizabeth Holden, was born to them at Gravois, on 21 October 1850. Mary Elizabeth died at Gravois on 22 Jun 1851, and her mother, Elizabeth, on 22 Aug 1851 most likely from cholera, which was endemic then.

A little of Michael Holden's history was later recounted by one of his daughters[199]:

> "...My father died when I was barely thirteen and I seem to have been the only one of the children who might have questioned him. He was ill three years before he passed on, and didn't care to talk much, but I know his parents died when he was a small boy and the two sisters who raised him were much older - old maids in fact. They apprenticed him to a wheelright[200] (sic) to learn that trade. It was the custom to sign a legal document that apprenticed the boy for seven years and during that time he lived right with his teacher and family. One of the tasks given him that was especially unpleasant was to clean the family shoes. He rebelled at this and ran away, but didn't dare go home, as his sisters would have brought him back. ....I would like to know how he existed till he was grown up, but he died before I got to questioning. "

Another person to take the trip was Ellen Peet (18 Feb 1823, Newborough, Lancaster, England). She reportedly had been married to Henry Isherwood

---

[199] Family letter from Anna Holden King to Helen Holden, 31 May 1934.
[200] The 1874 City Directory for Salt Lake City, Lists Michael Holden's occupation as "wagon maker".

(28 Apr 1816 - 24 Jul 1849, Toxteth Park, Lancashire, England) on 28 Jan 1849, but he died shortly thereafter.

The church elder, John Sutton, married Michael Holden and Ellen Peet at Gravois, Morgan County, MO on 23 Sep 1851; just a month after the death of Michael's first wife. The family story is that the church did not think that the two of them could survive the wagon trip to Salt Lake City separately and so had them marry. Physically, Ellen had fair skin and bright blue eyes. Michael was darker with black hair.

Michael and Ellen had the following children:

1. William Michael born about 2AM, 3 Sep 1853, Gravois, MO. Died 30 Sep 1853 at Gravois, MO.

2. Nephi Peet Holden born 1:30AM 23 Jun 1856 in SLC. Died 27 May 1916 in SLC of a heart attack. Nephi married Francis Elizabeth Ringwood on 17 May 1878. Their children included: Nephi Charles Frank Holden (15 Feb 1879-3 Oct 1930); Ethel Diana Holden (25 Sep 1880-20 Aug 1881); Gertrude Frances Holden (16 Sep 1890-Dec 1985); and Dora Holden (30 Jul 1892-30 Jul 1892).

3. Margaret Ellen Holden was born 2 AM 7 Sep 1858 in SLC. She died of consumption 30 Jan 1898 in SLC. She had a daughter named Beryl. Beryl in turn married Thomas Hormer and the two of them operated a real estate abstract office.

4. Michael William Holden, born [201] 6PM 28 Aug 1860 in SLC. (Continued.)

5. Thomas James Holden, born 8PM 3 Mar 1862 in SLC. Died 4 Jul 1863.

6. Anna Holden, born 4AM 2 Mar 1865 in SLC. Died 31 Aug 1953 in San Gabriel, CA[202]. Anna married Howard A. King on 10 Oct 1888. Their children included: Harold H. King (17 Jul 1889); Leslie Holden King (1893-1920); and Carol King (12 Oct 1899). Anna and Howard divorced 5 Feb 1919. Anna was elected to the Utah

---

[201] From family records of Helen Holden Mills. Although the 1900 Census for Yakima, lists his birth date as Aug 1859, the 3 Jun 1880 Census for Salt Lake City lists an age of 19, which is consistent with the birth date of 28 Aug 1860. Similarly, the 18 Aug 1870 SLC census lists his age as 9 and so the 28 Aug 1860 birth date is taken to be correct.

[202] She is buried in Salt Lake City Cemetery, SLC, UT. Plot 37, Block 1, Lot 3E.

legislature in 1912, where she served from 1913 to 1915. This was a very rare thing for a woman at that time. She also wrote poetry.

Michael Holden died in Salt Lake City, UT on 8 Mar 1879 of liver trouble. Ellen Peet died there the following year on 25 Dec 1880 with pneumonia[203].

4. Michael William Holden, son of Michael Holden and Ellen Peet, had a stuttering problem as a youth. He eventually outgrew it, but was shy and refused to go to school out of fear of being teased by the other boys of his age. He instead studied at home[204]. Michael Holden is listed on the 3 Jun 1880 Census as living with his mother in Salt Lake City; his occupation being laborer.

Michael Holden in Salt Lake City,
probably just prior to 1880:

---

[203] They are buried together at the Salt Lake City Cemetery, SLC, UT. Plot E, Block 2 Lot 10, S1/2.
[204] Spelling was also a problem for him. For example later as an adult, he is known to have spelled "Made" as "Maid".

This would have been about a year after his father's death and only about 6 months before his mother's. His sister later wrote, [205] "...As only the home had been left to mother and money owing, that she was never able to collect, it was necessary for him to find work and he went to Colorado with quite a group of young men. They were tricked in some way by a labor agent and had to scatter around finding work wherever they could and unable to get back to Salt Lake City.....". [206] He found some work at coalmines in Wyoming[207].

He dropped his given first name of "Michael" and took the name of "William Holden" or "William Victor Holden".

On 8 December 1889, William Holden and Mary "Mamie" Josephine Day were married by a Catholic Priest, Cyril Van der Donckt[208], at Malta, Idaho Territory. Mary had been born 14 Jan 1864. William's residence then was given as Hailey, ID [209]. Mamie was described [210] later by one of William's sisters as, "an interesting well educated woman, who had many social contacts." William had been raised as a Mormon, but Mary Day was a Catholic. In this situation, Father Van der Donckt presented William with an 1884 book on the Catholic faith, *"Catholic Belief"*, probably as part of a conversion effort. It, or most likely Mary [211], must have worked, as William remained a Catholic

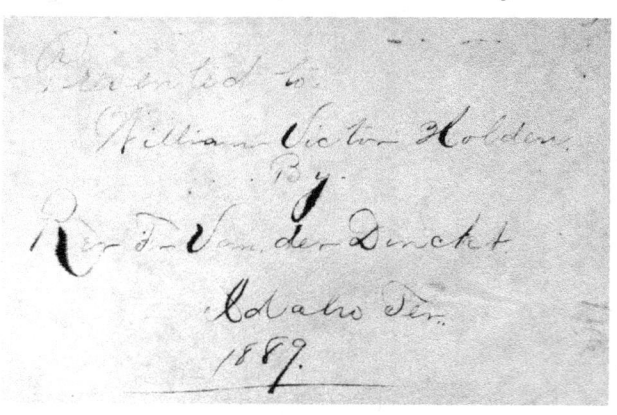

[205] Family letter from Anna Holden King to Helen Holden, 28 Jan 1935.

[206] There is a family story, and one that William almost certainly did tell to his children, that he had left home because his father had taken a second wife; something William did not agree with. Unfortunately, the research for this book could find no evidence to support this story; no second wife could be found.

[207] Told by Helen Holden.

[208] The priest had been born 1864 in Belgium in 1864 and came to Idaho in 1887 immediately after being ordained.

[209] On 2 July 1889 a fire destroyed almost all of the business district of Hailey Idaho. Rebuilding began almost immediately and it is possible that William Holden was there for the reconstruction effort.

[210] Family letter from Anna Holden King to Helen Holden, 28 Jan 1935.

[211] Given the lack of wear on the book.

the rest of his life.

They did not stay in Idaho, going almost immediately to Whatcom County in Washington. Washington had just received Statehood in Nov 1889.

On 21 Feb 1890 William V. Holden and Frank P. Miller purchased an acre of land on the shore of Drayton Harbor near Blaine for $300 from Watson Eastman[212]. They then mortgaged (sold) the property for $500 on 17 May 1890 to S. P. Hughes and A. D. McDonald (and their wives, Melissa and Charlotte). According to a promissory note, the $500 was to be paid by 18 Jul 1890; not a bad return on their investment.

At about the same time, 19 May 1890, William purchased a 40' by 100' lot from the Blaine Land Company for $50. It was Lot 3 in Block 35 of the Company's First Addition to Blaine"[213]. Family tradition is that William intended to build a home here for Mary. Events interfered with his plans, but the property's association with his wife seems to have been so strong that he could not bring himself to sell it in his lifetime. The property remained in the family for almost exactly a hundred years[214].

William Holden in New Whatcom, WA about 1892.

---

[212] Approximate location is 48.978481, -122.738636.
[213] Based on the Company's 1889 plat description, the lot was located on the east side of Fourteenth St., between E St. and F St. Approximate location is [48.996783, -122.73318].
[214] William's daughter, Ruth, sold the property to Dennis and Ann Olason on 4 Jan 1990.

William and Mary had a daughter, Anna A. Holden, born 21 Sep 1890. She died 22 Oct 1890 and was buried at Bayview Cemetery, Bellingham, WA in Section F, Lot 364, Grave #4 on 30 Oct 1890[215].

Monument for Anna A Holden

The markings on the cemetery monument read:

In memory of
ANNA A.
Infant Daug. of
WᴹV. & MARY J. HOLDEN
BORN
Sept. 21, 1890
DIED
Oct. 22, 1890
He carries the lambs in His
bosom

There is some hint that Anna may have had a twin sister. In addition to the records for Anna Holden, the Cemetery also recorded the burial of a

---

[215] As noted below, the Headstone for "Anna A. Holden" gives birth and death dates of 21 Sep 1890 and 22 Oct 1890. The cemetery records say that her death date was 20 Oct and that she was buried on 30 Oct 1890. Family records from Helen Holden Miles have slightly different dates, claiming that Anna was born on 28 Oct 1890 and died on 25 Nov 1890. In the absence of other clarifying records, the monument dates are taken as correct for this book.

separate infant daughter of William Holden in Section F, Lot 365, Grave #6. The cemetery records say that this infant died 28 Oct 1890 and was buried 2 Nov 1890. The Daily Reveille newspaper of New Whatcom, WA, and dated Thursday, 30 Oct 1890 reported, "An infant daughter of W.V. Holden died Tuesday (i.e. 28 Oct), and was interred at 3PM yesterday"; this was repeated on page 8 of the Bellingham Bay Reveille newspaper of Friday Oct 31, 1890. It is not clear why the cemetery records indicate the burial of two infants, when the family seems to have recognized only one. A physical examination of both gravesites might now be the only way to resolve this confusing data.

William Holden was listed in an 1890 New Whatcom City (now Bellingham) directory as "Holden, Wm V" where his occupation was indicated as laborer. He was living in town near the waterfront on Army Street near Holly Street. An 1891 Directory lists him as "Holden, W. V." living a little West of there, on Front Street (now Eldridge Ave.)

William and Mamie then moved to Yakima[216], WA. In the early 1880's Yakima was virtually a desert and needed water for its agricultural efforts. In response, a number of privately financed irrigation companies had been setup. One of the first was the Schanno Ditch Company that took water from the Naches River and directed it to the Yakima area. After moving to Yakima, William worked for this company before becoming a builder. He served as a ditch rider guarding the irrigation canal lines. His job included riding on horseback along the canal up to the Naches end of the canal and back again every day checking for any problems. His pay for this was about $30 per month.

Mamie J. Day Holden died in Yakima on Sunday night, 4 Dec 1898, "from the effects of an exhausting fever" [217]. She was 34 years old. Her funeral took place at the Catholic Church at 10:30 on Wednesday, 7 Dec 1898. She was probably buried initially at the cemetery in Union Gap, but she was

---

[216] Yakima City had been bypassed by the Northern Pacific Railroad with the nearest depot being located about 5 miles northwest of it. In response, much of the town (over 100 buildings) was moved North with rollers and horse teams to the site of the depot during the winter and spring of 1884/5. The "new" town was called North Yakima until 1918 when the name was changed to Yakima; the original town then becoming Union Gap, WA. Yakima, as used in this book, refers to the area of the current city.

[217] The Yakima Herald, 8 Dec 1898, p. 14. Family records of Helen Holden Mills confirm the death date. The cause of death was consumption (tuberculosis). This explains why William had moved to Yakima in the first place. He was deeply in love with his first wife and most likely moved to the dry climate of Yakima to try to provide for treatment of her disease. No antibiotics were available at that time and moving to a dry climate was often recommended.

moved to the Catholic Calvary Cemetery in Yakima when it opened in 1903[218].

Mary J. Holden's marker, Wm. Holden is buried to the left.

Why William and Mary had chosen Yakima as the place to go to is not known. One possibility, however, is that it might have been because of a Catholic priest, Father Jean Baptiste Boulet. He had come to New Whatcom and Sehome (now Bellingham) in 1889, just before the Holden's arrived, and started the Church of the Assumption. As the only priest there, Mary would certainly have met and known him. From 1868 to 1871 he had been in the Yakima area as a teacher for the Indian children and so was very familiar with its climate. He might well have suggested Yakima for Mary's illness.

William was listed as "W. V. Holden" on the 1900 census and was living at 345 Moxie Ave. in Yakima, WA. His occupation then was carpenter. By 1903 he was involved with local politics and was one of six representatives

---

[218] The grave is in Block C, Section 68, West 1/2, grave 5.

from the City's Third Ward to the city convention on 12 November[219]. In 1904 he was involved with local Republican Party politics and again was a delegate at the Yakima County convention on 27 Aug 1904.

William married secondly, Mary "Mollie" L. Brockett of Enfield, IL on 10 Aug 1905.

Mary's Brockett family has been in North America since the arrival of John Brockett in Boston on 26 Jun 1637. The history of the Brockett's has been well documented [220] and only the direct connection between him and her family is listed here:

1. John Brockett (ca 1610 - 12 Mar 1690, Wallingford, CT). Wife unknown.

2. Samuel Brockett (14 Jan 1652, New Haven, CT - 27 Oct 1742, Wallingford, CT). Wife was Sarah Bradley.

3. John Brockett (8 Nov 1685 - 12 Jan 1753 Wallingford, CT). Wife was Huldah Ells.

4. Elisha Brockett (31 May 1726 - 1805 Wallingford, CT). Wife was Sarah Stevens (Born 1725, NC).

5. William E. (Ebenezer) Brockett (26 Jun 1748 Wallingford, CT - 3 May 1821 Carthage, TN). Wife was Patsey (Martha J.) Ives. William served in the Revolutionary War and eventually reached the rank of Captain.

6. [221]William E. Brockett (Jr.) (24 Mar 1783, York Co., SC). Wife (#1) was Minerva Cartmill.

7. William B. (Benjamin) Brockett (16 Dec 1811, LA (or TN) - 29 Feb 1876 Brownsville, White County, IL). Wife was Irene (Ann) Jenkins (1816-1871).

---

[219] The Yakima Democrat newspaper of 7 Nov 1903 incorrectly listed his name as "H. V. Holden".

[220] See for example, The Descendants of John Brockett, One of the Original Founders of New Haven Colony, 1905, Edward J. Brockett.

[221] William B. Brockett and William E. Brockett (Jr.) are believed to be the father and grandfather of Michael S. Brockett. This differs from the genealogy that was prepared by Lorena Phelps Oberly in 1962 (unpublished family document) for Helen Holden, but the references of that document do not support its claims. Brockett researchers should verify this branch, if important for their work.

8. Michael S. Brockett, born 7 Mar 1839, Pope County, IL. Died 1921.

Michael S. Brockett was Mollie's father. He had served in the Civil War, as had one of his brothers, Matthew J. Brockett, born 1 Sep 1841 in White County, IL. They were members of the US 56th Illinois Volunteer Infantry Regiment. In Mar 1865 they were on board the ship General Lyon that had been chartered by the US Army for a passage from North Carolina to Norfolk, VA. On board were a little over 600 passengers composed of a large number of discharged Union soldiers returning home (including a 205-man contingent of the 56th Illinois Regiment), a number of Confederate prisoners of war, sixty refugees and other passengers. On 17 Mar 1865 the ship hit rough weather off Cape Hatteras, NC. A fire broke out in the engine room [222] and quickly spread through the ship. There were only 28 survivors. Of the 205-man Illinois Regiment, five survived [223]. Michael was one of those five, but his brother was not. He later related his story[224]:

> "When the fire broke out I was sleeping by the side of my brother. We were only 25 feet from the hatch. The flames spread so quickly that no alarm was given and I was badly burned before I was awakened. .....I grabbed a boat and pitched it into the sea and leaped in after it and several fellow soldiers followed suit. Three besides myself made fast on the boat. We drifted helplessly about at the mercy of the waves, expecting every minute to be our last...... After having spent nine hours on the sea, we were sighted by the steamer Gen. Sedgwick. A rope was thrown to our boat and I fastened it to my body; the other men were tossed ropes and the work of rescue was begun. The rough condition of the sea and the suction of the vessel carried me under and to the other side of the boat. In drawing me back, the crew used so much force that seven of my ribs were broken and I was otherwise uninjured..."

Following the war, he married first Elizabeth E. Draper[225] on 21 Oct 1865 in White County, IL.

---

[222] Possibly from a barrel of kerosene in the Porter's room being broken open by the storm and seeping down though the decks to the engine room where it ignited.

[223] The New York Times of 3 Apr 1865.

[224] See *National Tribune Repository, Vol 1, No. 4* for his complete version. If read critically, the full article suggests the possibility that he and his group may actually have made no attempt to rescue anyone else, but that assessment is left to the reader.

[225] The Yakima Marriage Register, 1891-1918, Vol 1, page 68 , for Mollie, incorrectly records the last name as "Graper".

Elizabeth E. Draper.

Michael S. Brockett as a young man.

An older Michael S. Brockett.

Elizabeth (Lizzie E.) Draper was born 2 Jan 1845 and died 11 Dec 1881. The 1880 Census for Enfield, White County, IL lists the Brockett family and their ages as:

Head:	M.S. Brockett	41
Wife:	Elizabeth E. Brockett	35
Dau:	Loly M. Brockett	14
Dau:	Laura E. Brockett	12
Dau:	Stella Brockett	10
Dau:	Lizzie A. Brockett	8
Son:	Jonah M Brockett	7 {4 Feb 1873 - 18 Feb 1951}
Son:	Willard M. Brockett	5
Dau:	**Mary L. Brockett**	**2 {born 7 Dec 1877}**
Dau:	Minnie Brockett	0

Michael S. Brockett remarried on 21 Oct 1891, about 10 years after the death of his first wife. His second wife, shown to the right, was Cynthia A. Robinson, a widow from Evansville, Indiana. Mary (Mollie) Brockett would have been almost 14 years old at this time. One of Cynthia's children from her second marriage (her first marriage had been to David Foster Henson) was Nellie Robinson, born about 1875, and so the two new stepsisters were of nearly the same age. The 1900 census shows that Mollie was living with her father, and "new" mother, but Nellie was no longer there. Mollie's occupation was listed as Teacher; she had attended Southern Illinois College in Enfield.

Mary (Mollie) L. Brockett as a young girl.

Mollie as young women in Enfield, IL

Michael Brockett farmed near Enfield, IL. A photo of his home, taken sometime after he had married Cynthia, is provided below:

Michael S. Brockett is on the far right. To the left of him (with white sleeves) is his son Willard L. Brockett. His son, Jonah Brockett is standing at the corner of the house in front of the dog. The lady to the left of Jonah is most likely Cynthia Brockett. The other family members have not been identified.

Mary Louella "Mollie" Brockett had first met William Holden in 1902 when she came to Yakima[226]. The reason she actually chose Yakima, and happened to meet William Holden, involves some interesting connections and concerns two attorneys. The first was Wesley Livsey Jones. Jones had graduated from Southern Illinois College, Enfield, IL. He went to Chicago and was admitted to practice law at the appellate courts there in the spring of 1886. In 1889 he came to Yakima and in 1890 started a law firm, "Rochford, Jones & Newman". (Jones later served as a US Senator from Washington State, 1909-1932, and died in office). The second was Wesley's half-brother, William P. Guthrie. Guthrie had also graduated from

---

[226] Family tradition, from Helen Holden and others, was that Mary had come to Yakima looking for a teaching position.

Southern Illinois College and earned a law degree at the University of Indiana in 1895. He came to Yakima on 23 Aug 1897 to join his half-brother's law firm. William P. Guthrie had married Nellie Robinson of Evansville, Indiana on 15 Aug 1897, just before coming to Yakima. In Yakima, Guthrie was a member of several fraternal organizations, one of them being the Woodmen of the World, Yakima Camp No. 89. William Holden was also a member of that organization and was even its manager[227]. Guthrie's wife, Nellie, was Mollie's stepsister. Accordingly, Mollie had originally come to Yakima to visit with her stepsister[228]. She met William Holden[229] almost certainly because of their common connections with William Guthrie.

William P. Guthrie moved his Practice to Twin Falls, Idaho in about 1904 and seems to have prospered there before returning and retiring in Yakima.

After her visit to Yakima, Mary had returned home to Enfield and so their romance must have been difficult. None-the-less, Mary came back to Yakima on a delayed train on Thursday 10 Aug 1905. She and William were married at 9PM that same evening at the parsonage of the Catholic Church[230]. Mary was a Presbyterian and so a marriage in the actual church would probably not have been allowed. They set up house at 208 N. Maxie Ave. (now N. Fifth Avenue) in Yakima. The house was expanded a number of times as the family grew and was part of the town's social scene. A local columnist, S.I. Anthon wrote, "Everyone of interest and merit has been entertained there." In spite of their age difference the couple did share interests in dancing, and playing whist and five-hundred, growing flowers and entertaining.

---

[227] *History of Klickitat, Yakima and Kittitas Counties, Washington*, 1904, Interstate Publishing Company, p.217.

[228] Another of Mollie's stepsisters, Mary (Henson) Barbour had moved to Edmonds, WA by 1910 and eventually ran a small grocery in Seattle. She was a daughter from Cynthia's first marriage to David Henson. Mary (also confusingly known as Mollie) kept in contact with Mollie Holden, as a sister, and as an aunt to the Holden daughters.

[229] William was an ardent Republican and later spent many Sunday afternoons under the maple trees at his home in discussion with Senator Wesley Jones and others. Another of William's friends was George Chalmers Goudy who, like Guthrie and Jones, had also been born in Enfield. George had married, Milda Nelson, the twin sister of the wife of Senator Jones. Helen Holden later recorded memories of Chalmer in his navy band uniform making music at the circular bandstand on the corner of North Fifth and West Yakima avenues.

[230] Edward E. Cleaver had obtained a marriage license for them earlier in the day.

Portraits of William Holden and Mollie Brockett as kept by their daughter, Lois.

They had three children:

1. Helen Beryl Holden born 29 May 1906. (Continued.)
2. Lois Pearl Holden, born 13 Jan 1909. (Continued.)
3. Ruth Elizabeth Holden, born 9 Jun 1915. (Continued.)

William continued in the construction trade. Many nights he and Molly (who had majored in math) would pore over blueprints and figure their bids. He oversaw construction of the St Elizabeth's Hospital building that opened on January 1, 1914. It was a five-story brick building at 110 S. 9th Avenue and served patients till 1963.

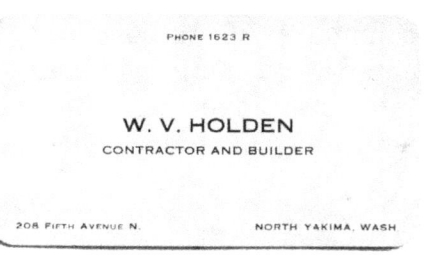

PHONE 1623 R

W. V. HOLDEN
CONTRACTOR AND BUILDER

208 FIFTH AVENUE N.   NORTH YAKIMA, WASH.

He built the Yakima Hardware Building, St. Paul's Parochial school, the Carmichael-Loudon house[231], the Garretson house at the top of Garretson's Grade, and many other structures in Yakima and surrounding areas.

St. Elizabeth's Hospital, Yakima Hardware, and St. Paul's School (left of Church)

---

[231] Located at 2 Chicago Ave; it is on the National Registry of Historic Places.

William also took up faming. He cleared land of volcanic rocks and established an apple orchard on 20 acres near Naches Heights[232]. He also seems to have raised some farm animals; in 1910, for example, he purchased a Duroc-Jersey swine, named "Rainbow" from D. B. Greenwalt, probably for breeding purposes[233].

In addition to his construction work, he gained income from some rental properties and the farm. In 1923, for example, he earned $183.48 for a house at 204 5th Avenue (on rent of $275), $270.02 for a house at 609 2nd Street (on rent of $420), and $282.07 in farm profits. Farm profits varied a bit, values for the last several crop years that he left records for were $1869.80 (1928), $1534.97 (1929), $624.87 (1930), and $1,107.22 (1931).

The depression ended the livelihood for William; his construction labor was no longer wanted and even the value of his apples was too low to justify picking.

Mollie had had a problem with her heart before the birth of her third daughter, Ruth and apparently was lucky to have survived it. She had a more serious attack around 13 Dec 1932; the doctors said the only thing to do was to go to bed and so she did through Christmas, New Years, and at least to the middle of January[234]. Mollie died[235] 4 Nov 1933, in the hospital William had built, and was buried at Terrace Heights Cemetery[236].

---

[232] The N1/2 of SW1/4 of NW 1/4 of Section 1 in Township 13 North, Range 17 East of the Willamette Meridian. The center of the property is about [46.646343, -120.653636].

[233] Duroc-Jersey Record Association, Volume 38, March 1911.

[234] In a letter dated 10 Jan 1933 and written," on the flat of my back" she lamented about not being able to go out and see the Christmas decorations on the town streets. She also noted, "Last night I could see the moon from my window. It was big and bright and friendly." {Her observation was correct in that the full moon that month occurred on 11 Jan.}

[235] From the heart problems.

[236] Block 10, Section 9, Lot 5 [approx. 46.61007, -120.46005]. Her marker also indicates that she was a member of the Royal Neighbors of America.

On 9 Jan 1940, William had his three daughters transfer all their interests in 4 city lots[237] and the farm property to him. This was part of the effort to finally close the probate actions resulting from the death of Mary Holden in 1933. The probate records showed that they and their father were heirs-at-law for her estate that consisted of those properties and which were valued at $9100[238]. On 7 Mar 1940, he sold the farm to George J. Marly and his wife Florence for $1800. Then on 12 Apr 1940 he allocated the 4 city lots back to his daughters by warranty deeds. Lois received Lot 2[239], Helen Lot 12, and Ruth Lots 3 and 4. He seems to have done this for two reasons. The first was probably to avoid the long probate as had been required for his wife Mary Brockett and secondly, to remove the farm property from his daughters[240].

William Victor Holden died on 20 Jun 1942 in Yakima WA   He is buried at the Catholic Calvary Cemetery in Yakima [241] next to his first wife. His family never installed a marker for him and only a plain concrete name block currently marks this location.

---

[237] Lot 12 in Block 44 of the City of Yakima, and lots 2, 3, and 4 in block 288 of Ker's second addition to Yakima.

[238] Claud Cissell, with Lloyd Wiehl and N. R. Blakey had been appointed by the court in 1939 to appraise the property of the estate. The appraised value was low enough that no estate taxes were due.

[239] Lois held the lot and house, at 204 North 5th Avenue, for some time before finally selling it on 8 Oct 1953 to Amy I. Curts for $2500.

[240] He did not believe that a woman would be able to operate the apple orchard and so sold it rather than leaving it to his daughters; to the lifelong consternation of at least one of them!

[241] William is buried in Block C, Section 68, West 1/2, grave 4, [46.5773,-120.538538]. Since Mollie Brockett, had not been a Catholic, she could not then be buried in that Cemetery with him.

1. Helen Beryl Holden, daughter of William V. Holden and Mary L. Brockett, was born 29 May 1906 in Yakima, WA. The photo is of Helen (age 4 months) with her mother. After High School in Yakima, Helen attended the University of Washington, earning a Bachelor of Music degree in Dec 1929 and also a degree in English. Seattle newspaper articles show that she was involved with the University's Varsity Ball that was held on 6 Dec 1929. She seems to have met her future husband, Francis Charles Mills at the University, as he was a student there in 1928, but it would be a long time, and after another romance for Helen, before they would marry.

After graduation, she taught English and music at Clover Park (near Tacoma). The Clover Park Junior High School district had just been formed in 1928. She was teaching there, in 1933 when her mother died. Condolences were sent by the faculty and also by two District members who would later have schools named after them: A. G. Hudtloff, Superintendent and Iva Alice Mann, District Secretary. Hudtloff's letter was on his personal stationary and ended with:

> "Do not worry about your school work. We will take care of it. We have a girl taking charge of you classes. I have sent your class book to you and if you will put the quarter grades in for each pupil we can take care of everything else.
>
> Many of the students have asked me to express their feeling of sympathy to you in you hour of sadness.
>
> Sincerely,
> A.G. Hudtloff"

Helen then taught at Easton High School[242], probably starting in the fall of 1934. Her father sent her a letter there early the next year:

> "208 No 5th Ave.
> Yakima Wash
> Feb 9 1935

Dear Helen

I received your letter yesterday. Glad to hear from you. Sorry you aren't so well. Hope you are better by this time. You ought to of stayed home out of the snow. You get hot then stand around and get cold. I have had the flu a week and a half but are over it now. The girls are all right. They are going to night school for typing. Lois is taking short hand lessons.

Laddy is all right, getting along fine. His hair won't come on till spring, then he will look all right. I think someone has poisoned some of my cats. One was awful sick yesterday and I have only seen one this morning.

I took the stove pipe down this morning before Ruth was up. Yes, I turn-on the radio on every night. I always get better sounds after 8, 9, or 10.

Well Helen, I am surprised you are going to get married I thought you was going to be an old maid. I am sorry tho' he ain't an Catholic. It makes lots of trouble some times after marriage and divorces, which makes life very unhappy. Of course you don't see that as I do as yet. As many a home is broken up over religion[243].

I don't know yet whether the girls will drive up to Easton - Sunday. They were talking about it, but they make so many changes. We have had lots of cloudy and foggy weather here lately. The sun is shinning today and it is fine. I don't think I go out to the ranch before the first.

With love and best wishes from all. Will close for this time,   Dad"

---

[242] The school was much smaller than Clover Park. It was in just one small building located on part of the area currently used for the school's tennis court.

[243] This marriage did not occur, but the reasons were probably other than religion.

It is not currently known who her fiancée was. It might have been the gentleman in this photo with Helen that was taken above the harbor in Tacoma, WA (ca. 1934); but she seems to have had a number of boyfriends.

In March 1936 Helen directed the Easton High School Orchestra on a program broadcast by the Seattle radio station KJR. They reportedly, "played popular tunes - and the latest at that."

In Dec 1937 she was accepted for a teaching position at Tekoa High School, SE of Spokane. She then returned to school herself and about Dec 1940 received a three-year normal teaching diploma from the University of Washington.

Helen and Francis Charles Mills finally married on 20 Jan 1940 in Yakima.

Helen continued her teaching career in Selah, Naches, Grandview, and Prosser where she taught English and Washington State History. She retired in 1976.

Francis Charles Mills had been born in Herne Hill, London, England 12 June 1909. In London he attended Rosendale Primary School and then Wilson's Grammar School (a school for boys). He came to the US with his family on 2 Sep 1921 and they settled in Kennewick, WA. He graduated from Kennewick High School in 1923 at age 14. He attended Washington State College in Pullman for one semester (1925-26) and then transferred to the University of Washington, earning a degree in chemistry in 1931. He started working for Pacific Power and Light in 1936 and spent his entire career with that company. In World War II, Francis was drafted and enlisted in Seattle on 15 Sep 1944 (S/N: 39480367). During the war he was stationed at Camp Crowder, MO. and Fort Monmouth, NJ, both Signal Corps Training Centers. He trained as an instructor in long distance telephone work, and was discharged as a Sergeant in 1946. Helen seems to have followed him around the country to most of the areas he was posted to. He enjoyed music and sang with a number of groups[244]. Most of his life he was also involved with local plays both as a performer and as a set builder; for example in May 1928 he performed as part of a reproduction of the original Olympic Games at the University of Washington's combined talent show and in 1976 he was the oldest actor in the outdoor presentation of "Trails West" in Walla Walla. Following Helen Holden's death, he remarried another "Helen" (Larson), whom he had met at work[245].

Francis's Cissell family nephews considered him a bit different from other family members. For example he would eat lemons[246] and had no trouble with over ripe bananas. He was frugal; in later years he would occasionally give moldy gifts of jams that he had canned years earlier resulting in comments like, "Oh well, it's just Francis". However, he could be counted on to do whatever task he thought was needed. For the RSVP program, he knitted over 1000 caps for the needy; some in University of Washington colors. He was a Boy Scout leader, taught swimming and life saving classes and enjoyed hiking[247], camping and fishing. He did not like hunting and would never touch a gun[248]. He did save a number of drowning victims and on at least one occasion was disturbed when made to stop life saving efforts early when he thought he might have been able to revive the person if given more time. The author can remember Francis carrying his old Collie dog "Jan" all the way home after she had died on a hike up in the hills above Terrace Heights near Yakima on one very hot summer day. Other memories are of Francis loading and carrying a 6-foot wooden pram on the top of his car so as to be able to stop along the way and do some fishing.

Francis did support Helen Holden in spending time and numerous holidays with her family. On the other hand, near her death, Helen had marked

---

[244] The groups included the Camp Crowder Concert Choir, the Schubert Club in Kennewick. Groups in Yakima included the Sun Barbershop group, the Yakima Symphony Chorus, and the Camerata Club.

[245] The family often referred to her as "Helen #2".

[246] Probably as a source for vitamin C.

[247] Francis was responsible for David Cissell and his brother Victor climbing Mt. Adams in the Cascades with him and a group from Yakima.

[248] This seemed to be a result of experiences during the war; he once told of training exercises with live ammunition being fired overhead while having to crawl across a field under barbed wire.

items with the names of people she wanted them to go to when she died. Francis did not comply with those requests and any Holden family items or records that Helen may have had were lost or destroyed.

Helen Holden died on 31 Jan 1982 in Walla Walla. She is buried at Terrace Heights Memorial Gardens[249] near Yakima and not too far from her mother. Francis Mills died on 11 May 1997 in Yakima.

2. Lois Pearl Holden, daughter of William V. Holden and Mary L. Brockett, was born 13 Jan 1909 in Yakima   Lois Holden graduated with the class of 1926-1/2 from Yakima High School and then attended Yakima Community College before finding work at Weber Chevrolet in Yakima.

Lois Holden, Formal Photo.   Lois about age 7

249 Block 41, Section 83, Lot 8. [approx. 46.610217,-120.460075].

Lois, Mollie and Ruth

Wm. Holden, Lois, Helen, Mollie Brockett (ca. 1932)

One of Lois's friends from High School was Charles "Charlie" Brown. He had graduated from Yakima High School in 1926 and so a half year before Lois. For some time he sent her photos with notes on the back, some of which she kept. One, for example, said:

> "There is water on the leaf.
> The grass is covered with dew.
> But just to be remembered,
> This I ask of you."

After high school, Charlie moved to Seattle with his family[250]. Hopefully this reference to him will provide the remembrance he asked of her.

3. Ruth Elizabeth Holden, daughter of William V. Holden and Mary L. Brockett, was born 9 Jun 1915 in Yakima.

She married first, George L. Allen, on 1 Aug 1935 in Yakima. The marriage ended with a divorce. They had a son, Michael Marcus Allen, who was born 26 Feb 1936 in Pasco, WA. Michael married Mildred (Millie) Ruth Kuegeman (born 4 Mar 1938, Los Angeles, CA) on 1 Aug 1959. Their Children were:

> 1. Terri Ann Allen, born 3 Aug 1965 in San Gabriel, CA. She married Richard Ross (born 11 Apr 1954, son of Alexander Ross and Eleanor Hayes) on 17 October 1987 in Marina del Ray, CA. Their children included:

> > 1-1. Brittany Nicole Ross, born 10 Dec 1989 in Riverside, CA.

> > 1-2. Cody Tucker Ross, born 2 Jun 1992 in Riverside, CA.

> 2. Lori Elizabeth Allen, born 18 Mar 1968 in San Gabriel, CA. She married Karl Werner Hick (born 3 Mar 1969). Their children included:

> > 2-1. Karl J. Hick, born 2001.

---

[250] Charles played high school football in 1925 and the school yearbook noted, "Eyes and complexion meant for a girl, yet he was a sportsman." In Seattle, Charles started a plastics fabrication company with his brothers, and married three times. He built a house on Lake Sammamish.

2-2. Camille Hick, born 2003.

Ruth married secondly, Elphage J. Mailloux on 28 Jun 1941 in Las Vegas, NV. Elphage was born 10 Jul 1913 in Yakima, WA and died 30 Oct 1956 in South Gate, CA. They had two children:

1. Craig Louis Mailloux, born at 8AM on 6 Apr 1943 in Inglewood, CA. Craig married Carol Joyce Schifferle (born 22 Aug 1942, daughter of Bobby Edward Schifferle and Evelyn Blanche Pate) on 9 Feb 1962 in Los Angeles, CA. Craig was a photographer for a number of news organizations including UPI[251]. He also had an interest in aviation and owned and flew his own plane. They had two daughters:

1-1. Karen Jean Mailloux, born 26 Aug 1962 in Burbank, CA.

1-2. Janet Kathleen Mailloux, born 3 Jul 1965 in Burbank, CA. Married Jay Alan Scherer 18 Mar 1990 in Denton TX.

2. Kim Holden Mailloux, born 15 Nov 1951 at St. Francis Hospital, Lynwood, CA. He married Victoria "Vicky" Jean Shubin (born 27 Jun 1951) on 12 Apr 1986 in Las Vegas, NV. Kim died in 2010 near Los Angeles, CA. Kim and Vicky had one daughter.

2-1. Jennifer Lynn Mailloux, born about 1981. Jennifer married George Samancioglu, born about 1978. Their children include.

2-1-1. Joshua Odin Samancioglu, born 8 Feb 2003 in Tarpon Springs, FL.

2-1-2. A daughter.

---

[251] During a visit to Craig's home the author's wife was surprised to see an image of her uncle, Odon Skupen, included in one of Craig's more famous news photographs displayed on a wall. As part of his news coverage, Craig had taken a photo of Charles Manson being lead to court; Odon was a Los Angeles County deputy sheriff and happened to be escorting Manson on the day the photo was taken.

Ruth and her children:

Craig Mailloux, Michael Allen, Ruth Holden. Kim Mailoux, in front.

Ruth married thirdly, Clarence Joseph Formaneck on 26 Jul 1975 in Las Vegas, NV. Clarence was born 11 Feb 1910 in Los Angeles, CA and died 9 Mar 1997, San Bernardino, CA.

Craig Mailloux, Carol Schifferle, Michael Allen, Mildred Kuegeman, George Samancioglu, and Jennifer Mailloux. The children are Joshua Samancioglu and his sister. (Abt. 2011)

Ruth died 24 Oct 1994 in San Bernardino County, CA and is buried alone at Desert Lawn Memorial Park, Calimesa, CA. [252]

---

[252] [33.95633,-117.022942]. The marker's death date is off by 1-day.

Historical Holden Family Photo:

The identity of this photo remains to be determined. It is documented here because it was of importance to either William Holden or Mollie Brockett. It was originally taken on a glass slide negative. Somehow the negative was broken, at which point the family had another negative made of the two broken pieces; indicating its value to them. This may be related to Mollie's family, but also might be of William's first wife or other Holden relative.

11. The Bluffton and Crossfield Cissells

There were two other Cissell families that also came to Alberta. These were generally located near the towns of Bluffton and Crossfield.

The first was the George Leonard Cissell family. They were a Catholic family and came to Canada from Louisville Kentucky about 1913. George had been born 28 Aug 1887 in New Hope, KY. He was the son of Henry (Sebastian) Cissell and Ruth D. (Hagen).

George was a descendent of person 7-1. James Cissell (see page 13) in the following manner:

7-1. James Cissell born by 1717 in St. Mary's County, MD and died 1785. Married Elizabeth _____.{or Margaret Vowels}

Ignatius Cissell, son of James Cissell and Elizabeth. Born in St. Mary's County, MD. Married Elizabeth ____in St. Mary's County MD. Ignatius was one of the 25 members of the Maryland League who emigrated to the Pottinger's Creek settlement in KY in 1785. He died ca 1788 in Nelson County, KY.

James Rudolph Cissell, son of Ignatius Cissell and Elizabeth. Born 22 May 1768, died ca 1830 in Washington County, KY. Married Susannah Williams Hammett on 7 Apr 1806 in Nelson County KY.

John Jefferson Cissell, son of James Cissell and Susannah Williams Hammett. Born 7 Dec 1807 in Nelson County, KY and died 10 May 1875 in Holy Cross, Marion County, KY. He married Letitia A. Clayton, daughter of John Clayton and Maria Hayden, on 11 Mar 1851.

Henry Sebastian Cissell, son of John Jefferson Cissell and Letitia A. Clayton. Born 25 Aug 1850 in Marion County, KY and died 10 Oct 1917 in Nelson County, KY. Married Dorothy Ruth Hagen, daughter of Thomas Sidney Hagen and Mary Amanda Edelen.

George Leonard Cissell, son of Henry Sebastian Cissell and Dorothy Ruth Hagen.

George had married Agnes Nevitt on 11 Jul 1911 in Jefferson County, KY. In Oct 1918, according to his WWI draft card, they were living in Rimbey, AB. He had grey eyes and light brown hair. His land grant may have been in Section 16, Township 44, Range 3 West of the 5th Meridian (W5M). The family lived for a few years on the Wagner farm, the NE 1/4 of Section 12, Township 43 Range 3 W5M. George worked for Mel Sheppard every fall on the threshing rig while living there. The couple spent their last days at Winfield, AB. Mary Agnes (1889-1966) is buried in the St. Mary's Catholic Cemetery, Bluffton, AB. George (1887-1972) is also buried there[253]. They had 8 Children:

1. Ruth Cissell, born about 1912 in the US.

2. Louise (Lucille) Cissell, born about 1912 in the US.

3. Walter Cissell, born about 1914 in Alberta, (but the 1916 census may say US.)

4. Leo Cissell, born about 1917 in Alberta.

5. John Cissell, born about 1919 in Alberta. He died in 1954 and is buried in Grande Prairie.

6. Gladys Cissell, born 1921 in Alberta.

7. Dorothy Cissell.

8. George Cissell.

---

[253] [52.711638, -114.292381].

The second family began with Bernard Joseph Cissell, a Catholic, who came to Ponoka alone in 1914. Bernard was a younger brother of George Leonard Cissell and had been born in 1895. The 1916 census shows him in Township 44, Range 2, W5M.

Bernard married Alice Edith Fleming in 1917 in Ponoka. Alice, the daughter of Louis and Alice Fleming, had been born Jul 1891 in Colby[254] Kansas. In 1900 her family was in Forest City, Sarpy County, Nebraska, but in 1903 Alice and her family moved to Ponoka.

Bernard and Alice spent much of the early part of their marriage in the Bluffton area, where Bernard was one of the early members of the Alberta Wheat Pool and a member of the school board. Bernard and Alice bought the SE 1/4 of Section 17, Township 42, Range 26, W4M (known as the Palmer Farm) in 1919. They sold the property in 1925. They got it back in 1927, rented the land to Alice's brother, Frank Fleming, for a few years and then resold it.

In 1943 they moved to the Crossfield district. In 1962 they retired to Edmonton. In the spring of 1964, they returned to the country and built a small home on the SW corner of Section 33. They were very active working about their place and Bernard was always a willing hand to help his neighbors fix fence, chase cattle or whatever came up. There was always a cup of tea for anyone who dropped in. In April 1969, the farm was sold to Ben Seiben. Bernard and Alice then moved to the Rocky View Lodge in Crossfield.

Bernard Joseph Cissell died in Mar 1973[255]. Alice died 6 Sep 1973. They are buried in the family plot at the Forest Home Cemetery, Ponoka[256].

Bernard and Alice had 10 Children:

1. Donald B. Cissell of Grand Prairie. Born 8 May 1919 and died 22 Feb 2009. Buried at Grande Prairie Municipal Cemetery.

2. Helen Cissell. Married Svend Larson of Ft. Saskatchewan. Died before 2010.

---

[254] As reported in her published obituary.

[255] Bernard's obituary indicated that several Louisville, Kentucky family members survived him. These included his brother Hagen Cissell and sisters Mrs. Mary Cecil, and Mrs. Nellie Boone.

[256] Joseph Bernard Cissell is in Block 7, Lot 144, Plot 3 and Alice Edith Cissell in Block 7, Lot 144, Plot 4. [52.678086,-113.609083]

3. Gordon Cissell of Edmonton. Born 3 March 1923, died 10 Dec 2010. Married Bernice _____ about 1947. During WWII he served in North Africa and Sicily. From 1956 to 1976 he ran his own company, B&C Coverings. Children included:

    3-1. Wayne Cissell. Married ____.

    3-2. Allan Cissell. Married ____.

4. Paul Cissell of Edmonton. Married Elsie _____.

5. Leonard Wilfred "Len" Cissell. Born 11 Mar 1932 and died 4 Dec 2011 in Edmonton. Married Michalene "Mickey" _____. Children included:

    5-1. Brian Cissell. Married Anne ____.

    5-2. Sheila Cissell.

6. Bernice Cissell. Married Arnold Linder of Edmonton. Died before 2010.

7. Delbert Joseph Cissell, born 18 Apr 1925 died 13 Jan 1926[257].

8. Joseph Leonard Cissell, born 20 May 1928 and died 1 Jul 2012. Married Victoria _____ about 1949. Victoria had been born in 1931 and died 12 Nov 2012. Lived in Crossfield, AB. Children included:

    8-1. Arlene Cissell. Married John Nouwen.

    8-2. Betty Cissell. Married Harry Chaba. They had at least one child:

        7-2-1. Brian Chaba, died in 1995.

    8-3. Carol Cissell. Married _____ Hebert.

    8-4. Kathy Cissell. Married Ken Smith.

    8-5. Robert Cissell. Married _____. Children included:

---

[257] Joseph Delbert Cissell is buried at the Forest Home Cemetery, Ponoka in Block 2, Lot 273, Plot 1.

7-5-1. Eric Cissell.

9.   Bernard Louis Cissell, born 1933. Married Beatrice _____.
Lived in Crossfield, AB. Children included:

9-1. Peter Cissell. Born 1969.

10. James Cissell, died as an infant on 24 Nov 1934[258].

Bernard and Alice Cissell

---

[258] Baby James Cissell, who died on 24 Nov 1934, is buried at St. Mary's Catholic
Cemetery near Bluffton, AB.

12. Family DNA Testing

For well over a hundred years there have been a number of Cissell family questions that could not be definitively answered because of the paucity of surviving written records from the 1500's and 1600's.

The following are examples of types of questions involved:

1. Since the Cissells of St. Mary's County were Catholics and the Cecil's of Prince George's County, MD were Protestants, it has seemed very unlikely that they were related. Is this assessment correct?

2. Many genealogists have claimed, and still do, that the Cissells of St. Mary's County were descended from William Cecil, Lord Burghley, and Secretary of State for Queen Elizabeth I. No records to prove this have been found, so is there really any such connection? Given that John Cissell was illiterate and that the Burghley's were extremely well educated, Burghley even being Chancellor of Cambridge University, this seems very unlikely.

3. What is the relationship, if any, between the Cissells (& Cecil's) of Maryland and the Cecil's of Philadelphia? This is of interest, because, unlike the two Maryland family groups, the English origins of Cecil Family in Philadelphia are known (Combe, Oxfordshire).

DNA testing offers a way to try to answer these types of questions, even when paper records cannot be found. One approach is to use the Y-Chromosome. This is passed, usually unchanged, from father to son. A son's Y-Chromosome then is almost identical to that of his father, grandfather, great-grand father, etc.

The genetic code on DNA and on the Y-Chromosome is composed of 4-letters: A, T, C, and G. At various locations along the Y-Chromosome there are sections where short sequences of DNA (normally 2-5 letters long) are repeated a certain number of times. This is almost like the DNA stuttering a bit while it was being copied. These sections are called "Short Tandem Repeats (STRs)". Each known STR has been given a name. One of these, as an example, is called DYS19[259]. At this location on the Y-chromosome the letter combination "TAGA" is repeated for a number of times. In one person it might be repeated 12 times, in someone else 14 times or perhaps 11 times, etc. Whatever repeat pattern a father might have, he transmits that same pattern to his son. {For Cissells it is repeated 15 times.}

Y-DNA testing can look for the known STRs and report the number of repeats found at each of these "markers". This allows for a comparison between individuals and a determination as to how closely related they may be. As this book is written, full DNA sequencing is unfortunately not yet available at practical cost, and so the STR type testing is all we can really use.

To answer question 1 above, two descendents of the original John Cissell (died 1698) from St. Mary's County and a descendent of the Prince George's County Cecils were tested. It was found that all three matched very closely. This implies that both groups are, in fact related. The DNA results mean that both the Prince George's County Cecils and the Cissells of St. Mary's County are related and do share a common male ancestor.

William Cecil, Lord Burghley, had two sons; one from each of his two wives. His oldest son, Thomas Cecil, attained the title of "Earl of Exeter" and that title has continued to today. To help answer question 2, a known descendent of Thomas Cecil agreed to do DNA testing. His results turned out to be very similar to those of the three Maryland Cissell descendents. This means that both the St. Mary's County Cissells and the Prince George's County Cecils are related to Lord Burghley in some way. They (and the Yakima and Ponoka Cissells) do share a common male ancestor with the family of Thomas Cecil and thus also his Father, Lord Burghley. Given the educational differences, it still seems unlikely that the Maryland Cissells are direct descendents of Lord Burghley, but the common male ancestor could have been Lord Burghley's grandfather, great grandfather, etc. The DNA results suggest that this common ancestor might have been in the 1400's or 1500's, but more testing would be needed to better ascertain the real date.

Question 3 can be answered with DNA testing. One quick attempt to find a descendent of the Pennsylvania (Philadelphia) Cecil family was made and a DNA test performed. This individual did not match either the Maryland

---

[259] For this marker, the "D" implies Double Stranded DNA, the "Y" implies Y-Chromosome, and the "S", Short Tandem Repeat. Not all marker names are this simple, many being very esoteric and well beyond the intent of this book.

Cissell or Lord Burghley family DNA results. This indicates that the Cecil family from Combe, Oxfordshire was not related to the other families in this book.

The following line[260] was used for this test and is provided for reference:

1. William Cecil, born before 1755 and died 1812 in Allegheny County, PA is taken to be the grandson (or great grandson) of the original William Cecil who came from Combe to Philadelphia with William Penn. He wife was Mary.

2. Charles Cecil, son of William and Mary was born ca 1785 in Allegheny County, PA and Married Naomi Eoff in Wheeling, WV. Charles died before 1840 in WV.

3. Charles Brower Cecil, son of Charles and Naomi Cecil, was born 2 Feb 1827 in Wheeling WV and died there 24 Aug 1873. He married Anna K. McFarland.

4. James McFarland Cecil, son of Charles and Anna Cecil, was born 25 Aug 1855 in Wheeling, WV. He married Bessie D. _____.

5. Charles Lee Cecil, son of James and Bessie Cecil, was born 16 May 1888 in WV. He married Genevieve Lyon.

6. Lee McFarland Cecil, son of Charles and Genevieve Cecil, was born 4 Sep 1925 in MN and died 10 Jun 1968, Marlin County, CA. He married Lillian Sigan.

7. A son of Lee Cecil and Lillian Sigan provided the DNA sample.

The actual test results are listed below for historical reference. "Exeter" is the descendent of the Earl of Exeter; SMC-1 and SMC-2 are the descendents of John Cissell (died 1698) of St. Mary's County Maryland; and Penn-1 is the Pennsylvania Cecil descendent. The values marked in bold numbers and underlined are those that differ from the DNA of the Earl of Exeter's descendent.

---

[260] Although the genealogy done to identify the Pennsylvania descendent is believed to be correct, it did not review all primary records. Any Pennsylvania Cecil family researcher should, therefore, verify this genealogy before formally accepting these results.

Marker	Exeter	SMC-1	SMC-2	PGC-1	Penn-1
DYS393	13	13	13	13	13
DYS390	23	23	23	23	**_25_**
DYS19	15	15	15	15	**_14_**
DYS391	10	10	10	10	**_11_**
DYS385	11-14	11-14	11-14	11-14	11-**_15_**
DYS426	13	13	13	13	**_12_**
DYS388	12	12	12	12	12
DYS439	13	13	13	**_12_**	**_11_**
DYS389i	13	13	13	13	13
DYS392	13	13	13	13	13
DYS389ii	29	29	29	29	29
DYS458	16	16	16	16	**_19_**
DYS459	9-10	9-10	9-10	9-10	9-10
DYS455	11	11	11	11	11
DYS454	11	11	11	11	11
DYS447	24	24	24	24	**_25_**
DYS437	15	15	15	15	15
DYS448	19	19	19	19	19
DYS449	27	27	27	27	**_29_**
DYS464	14-14-17-17	14-14-**_14_**-17	14-14-**_16_**-17	14-14-17-17	**_15-15-_**17-17
DYS460	10	10	10	10	10
Y-GATA-H4	11	**_10_**	11	11	11
YCAII	19-23	19-23	19-23	19-23	19-23
DYS456	15	15	15	15	15
DYS607	15	15	15	15	**_14_**
DYS576	17	17	17	17	**_16_**
DYS570	17	17	17	17	**_18_**
CDY	37-38	37-38	37-38	37-38	**_36-39_**
DYS442	12	12	12	12	12
DYS438	12	12	12	12	12
DYS531	11	11	11	11	
DYS578	9	9	9	9	
DYF395S1	15-16	15-16	15-16	15-16	
DYS590	8	8	8	8	

DYS537	10	10	10	10
DYS641	10	10	*__11__*	10
DYS472	8	8	8	8
DYF406S1	10	*__11__*	*__11__*	10
DYS511	10	10	10	10
DYS425	0	0	0	0
DYS413	23-23	23-23	23-23	23-23
DYS557	17	*__16__*	*__16__*	*__16__*
DYS594	10	10	10	10
DYS436	12	12	12	12
DYS490	12	12	12	12
DYS534	15	15	15	15
DYS450	8	8	8	8
DYS444	12	12	12	12
DYS481	23	23	23	23
DYS520	20	20	20	20
DYS446	13	13	13	13
DYS617	12	12	12	12
DYS568	11	11	11	11
DYS487	13	13	13	13
DYS572	11	11	11	11
DYS640	11	11	11	11
DYS492	13	13	13	13
DYS565	12	12	12	12
DYS710	33	33		*__32__*
DYS485	15	15		15
DYS632	9	9		9
DYS495	16	16		16
DYS540	12	12		12
DYS714	28	28		28
DYS716	26	26		26
DYS717	19	19		19
DYS505	13	13		13
DYS556	11	11		11
DYS549	12	12		12
DYS589	12	12		12
DYS522	10	10		10
DYS494	9	9		9
DYS533	12	12		12
DYS636	12	12		12
DYS575	10	10		10
DYS638	11	11		11
DYS462	11	11		11
DYS452	30	30		30
DYS445	12	12		12
Y-GATA-A10	12	12		12
DYS463	24	24		24

Family DNA Testing

DYS441	13	13	13
Y-GGAAT-1B07	10	10	10
DYS525	10	10	10
DYS712	20	19	20
DYS593	15	15	15
DYS650	18	18	18
DYS532	13	13	13
DYS715	24	24	24
DYS504	17	17	17
DYS513	12	12	12
DYS561	15	_**16**_	15
DYS552	24	24	24
DYS726	12	12	12
DYS635	23	23	23
DYS587	18	18	18
DYS643	10	10	10
DYS497	14	14	14
DYS510	17	17	_**18**_
DYS434	9	9	9
DYS461	12	12	12
DYS435	11	11	11

13. Overall Family Tree

Most of the descendents of the John Cissell (1698) of St. Mary's County MD and who are mentioned in this book are listed below so as to show their location in the overall family tree:

1 John CISSELL (abt 1638 England – 1698 St. Mary's Co, MD)
+ Mary UKN
  2 John CISSELL
  2 William CISSELL
  2 Thomas CISSELL
  2 Richard CISSELL
  2 Robert CISSELL
  2 Edward CISSELL
  2 James CISSELL (– abt 1717 St. Mary's Co, MD)
   + Mary
    3 James CISSELL (– abt 1785 St. Mary's Co, MD)
     + Elizabeth
      4 Ignatius CISSELL (1734 St. Mary's Co, MD – 1788 Nelson Co, KY)
       + Elizabeth (– 1798)
        5 Bennett CISSELL (1756 –)
        5 Edmund CISSELL (1760 – 1782)
        5 James Rudolph CISSELL (22 May 1768 – 1830)
         + Susannah Williams HAMMETT
          6 John Jefferson CISSELL (7 Dec 1807 – 10 May 1875, KY)
           + Letitia A. CLAYTON
            7 Henry Sebastian CISSELL (25 Aug 1850 – 10 Oct 1917, KY)
             + Dorothy Ruth "Dee" HAGAN (13 Aug 1853 of KY –)
              8 George Leonard CISSELL (28 Aug 1887, KY – 1972 Winfield, AB)
               + Agnes NEVITT
                9 Ruth CISSELL (abt 1912 –)
                9 Louise (Lucille) CISSELL (abt 1912 –)
                9 Walter CISSELL (abt 1914 AB –)
                9 Leo CISSELL (abt 1917 AB –)
                9 John CISSELL (abt 1919 AB –)
                9 Gladys CISSELL (1921 AB –)
                9 Dorothy CISSELL
                9 George CISSELL
              8 Bernard Joseph CISSELL (1895 of KY – 1973 Alberta, Canada)
               + Alice FLEMMING (Jul 1891 of Colby, KS –)
                9 Donald B. CISSELL (8 May 1919 AB – 22 Feb 2009 AB)
                9 Helen CISSELL (– bef 2010)
                 + Svend LARSON
                9 Gorden CISSELL (3 Mar 1923 AB – 10 Dec 2010)
                 + Bernice UKN
                  10 Wayne CISSELL
                  10 Allan CISSELL
                9 Paul CISSELL

```
                    + Elsie UKN
                  9 Leonard Wilfred CISSELL (11 Mar 1932 – 4 Dec 2011, AB)
                    + Michalene (Mickey) UKN
                      10 Brian CISSELL
                        + Anne UKN
                      10 Sheila CISSELL
                  9 Bernice CISSELL ( – bef 2010)
                    + Arnold LINDER
                  9 Delbert Joseph CISSELL (18 Apr 1925 AB – 13 Jan 1926)
                  9 Joseph Leonard CISSELL (20 May 1928 AB – 1 Jul 2012)
                    + Victoria UKN (1931 – 12 Nov 2012)
                      10 Arlene CISSELL
                        + John NOUWEN
                      10 Betty CISSELL
                        + Harry CHABA
                          11 Brian CHABA ( – 1995)
                      10 Carol CISSELL
                        + Ukn HERBERT
                      10 Kathy CISSELL
                        + Ken SMITH
                      10 Robert CISSELL
                        + (Name Unknown)
                          11 Eric CISSELL
                  9 Bernard Louis CISSELL (1933 of Alberta, Canada – )
                    + Beatrice UKN
                      10 Peter CISSELL (1969 of Alberta, Canada – )
                  9 James CISSELL (1934 AB – 24 Nov 1934)
        5 Ignatius Jr. CISSELL (1764 – 1831)
        5 Joseph CISSELL (1766 – 1827)
          + Susanna Clarke (1770 – 1840)
            6 Lewis CISSELL (1794 – 1842)
            6 Elizabeth CISSELL (1795 – 1859)
            6 Mary CISSELL (1799 – 1860)
            6 Joseph CISSELL (1802 – 1860)
            6 George CISSELL (1804 – 1863)
              + Mary June Gilkey (1804 – 1873)
                7 William A CISSELL (1827 – 1870)
                  + Elizabeth Downs (1826 – 1880)
                    8 Margaret Jane CISSELL (1852 – 1875)
                    8 George Walton CISSELL (1854 – 1929)
                      + Elizabeth "Betty" BURNS (1833 – 1896)
                        9 Alphonses "Fonzie" CECIL (1874 – 1926)
                        9 Bernard Alexander CECIL (1876 – 1944)
                        9 William Linus CECIL (28 Jul 1878, KY – 26 May 1969, KY)
                          + Susan WILETT (7 Apr 1889 – )
                            10 Joseph Earl CECIL (8 Jun 1908 – )
                              + Mary Agnes LYVERS (16 May 1910 – 3 Sep 1989)
                                11 Ramey Harold CECIL (8 Nov 1929 New Hope, KY – )
                                  + Laura Ann YATES (20 Aug 1932 Dickson, TN – )
                                    12 Randle Harold CECIL (Nov 1950, TN – Feb 2001, KY)
                                      + Pamela Victoria MILLIKEN (19 Aug 1950, TN – )
                                        13 Jason Andrew CECIL (abt 1970 Lexington, KY )
                                    12 Julia CECIL (1952 – )
```

11 Elizabeth Jean "Betty" CECIL (1931 –)
11 Robert Earl CECIL (1932 –)
11 Charles Bernard CECIL (1943 –)
11 Joyce Marie CECIL (1945 –)
11 Ann Simmon CECIL (1947 –)
11 Patricia Josephine CECIL (1949 –)
11 Joseph Glenn CECIL (1951 –)
11 Francis L? CECIL (1952 –)
10 Willett CECIL
10 Ruby CECIL
10 Gladys CECIL
10 Rollie CECIL
10 Billy CECIL
10 Ben CECIL
10 Mary Bryant CECIL
10 Raymond "R V" CECIL
10 Anna Faye CECIL
10 Margie CECIL
8 Frances Catherine CISSELL (1856 – 1857)
8 Thomas CISSELL (1858 – 1873)
8 William Monroe CISSELL (1860 – 1880)
8 Mary Teresa CISSELL (1863 –)
8 John CISSELL (1865 –)
8 Anna Isabelle CISSELL (1868 –)
7 James R CISSELL (1829 – 1916)
7 Cecilia James CISSELL (1830 – 1852)
7 Mary Catherine CISSELL (1831 – 1868)
7 Susan Margaret CISSELL (1835 – 1911)
7 Joseph Owen CISSELL (1837 – 1900)
4 Francis CISSELL
4 Bennett CISSELL
4 Bernard CISSELL (12 Feb 1759 St. Mary's Co, MD – 4 Jul 1833 Perry Co, MO)
 + Monica PAYNE (13 Mar 1763 Leonardtown, MD – 3 Feb 1837 Perry Co, MO)
  5 Lewis CISSELL (abt 1784 St. Mary's Co, MD – Jun 1858 Perry Co, MO)
  5 Mary J. CISSELL (abt 1786 KY – 11 Jul 1835 Perry Co, MO)
   + Simon DUVALL
    6 Lewis/Louis DUVALL
    6 Sarah DUVALL
    6 Mary DUVALL
    6 Elizabeth DUVALL
    6 Theresa DUVALL
    6 Joseph DUVALL
    6 Simon C. DUVALL
    6 Clement S. DUVALL
    6 John Chrysostom DUVALL
    6 Ann Arpy (Lucy) DUVALL
    6 Rosa(lia) DUVALL
    6 Thomas P. S. DUVALL
  5 Clement CISSELL (15 Oct 1789 KY – 15 May 1859 Perry Co, MO)
   + Anne LAYTON
    6 Mary CISSELL
    6 Elizabeth CISSELL
    6 Catherine CISSELL

      6 Theresa CISSELL
      6 Leo CISSELL
      6 Mary Ann CISSELL
      6 Helena CISSELL
      6 Isadore CISSELL
      6 Hillary CISSELL
    5 Joseph CISSELL (abt 1792 KY – abt 1880 Perry Co, MO)
     + Ann MILES
      6 Mary Martina CISSELL (abt 1817 Perry Co, MO – abt 1880)
       + Raymond TUCKER
      6 Narius CISSELL (abt 1819 Perry Co, MO – Dec 1877 Perry Co, MO)
       + Christina HAGAN
        7 Nerius (Martin) CISSELL (18 Jan 1842, MO – 19 Mar 1906, Ponoka)
         + Elizabeth E (Alice Mary) BEY (8 Oct 1847 – 14 Jul 1924, Yakima)
         8 Leon Albert CISSELL (abt 29 Jun 1867, MN – 3 Jul 1915, Ponoka)
          + Clara May THORSNESS (1874, MN – 11 Sep 1913, AB)
          9 William Arthur CISSELL (14 Feb 1896 – 19 Apr 1960, WA)
           + Dorra EMERSON (17 Jun 1905 – 7 Jul 2006)
          9 Ernest Leon CISSELL (3 Jan 1897 – 5 Feb 1965 Olympia, WA)
           + Lois HOLLOWAY (10 Feb 1904 – 21 Feb 2002 Olympia, WA)
          10 Richard L. CISSELL (16 Sep 1930 – 17 May 2006, WA)
           + Nelda Ann BRACY (1 May 1940 Olympia, WA –)
           11 Leann Marie CISSELL (28 Jan 1962 Olympia, WA –)
            + Frank Anthony CARANCI (26 Mar 1948 , PA –)
            12 Samantha Paige CARANCI (16 Jul 1996, WA –)
            12 Daniel CARANCI (15 Aug 1998 Olympia, WA –)
            12 Ivy Marie CARANCI (16 Jun 1999 Olympia, WA –)
           11 Lori Jean CISSELL (17 Feb 1963 Olympia, WA –)
           11 Lucia Ernestine CISSELL (12 Jan 1970 Olympia –)
            + Lennie E. THEDE (6 Dec 1971 –)
            12 Luca Alexander THEDE (30 Oct 2006, WA –)
          10 Lois Jean CISSELL (13 Mar 1939 – 6 Nov 2005, WA)
         9 Claud Richard CISSELL (5 Dec 1898 – 14 Oct 1965, WA)
          + Lois Pearl HOLDEN (13 Jan 1909 – 6 Sep 1982, WA)
          10 David CISSELL (27 Feb 1945 Tacoma, Pierce, WA –)
           + Julie ZALIKOWSKI (11 Jul 1953 Arvada, CO –)
          10 Victor CISSELL (25 Oct 1946 Yakima, Yakima, WA –)
           + Judith Emalyne Swenson CARLSON (18 Aug 1948 –)
           11 Amy Ellen Carlson CISSELL (1 Oct 1975 –)
            + Robert DROESSLER
            12 Quinten Harold DROESSLER (29 Mar 2010, WA –)
            12 Emmitt Lee DROESSLER (8 Mar 2012, WA –)
            12 Cora Eileen DROESSLER (8 Mar 2012, WA –)
           11 Chad Holden CISSELL (12 Dec 1983 Puyallup, WA –)
          + Judy EAGLE (9 Apr 1946 –)
          10 Stephen CISSELL (8 Sep 1951 Tacoma, WA –)
           + Carol Louise KINNUNE (29 Dec 1951 –)
           11 Ashley Elizabeth CISSELL (11 Nov 1980, WA –)
            + Humphrey _____
            12 Kali CISSELL (22 Aug 2005 Bellevue, WA –)
            + Gregory Thomas TALECK
            12 Miles Owen TALECK (27 Sep 2011, CA –)
            12 Sierra Madison TALECK (21 Sep 2013, WA –)

11 Ryan Paul CISSELL (7 Mar 1985 Bellevue, WA –)
  + Eugénie VILLERONCE (18 Jun 1986 Marseille -)
    12 Léonie Marie CISSELL (18 Aug 2014 Bellevue, WA –)
+ Kim PULLIAM
+ Villette Teresa NOLON
9 Albert Lewis CISSELL (21 Nov 1900, SD – 26 Apr 1945, WA)
 + Dollie TURNER (abt 1909 NY – Oct 1975 Belen, NM)
  10 James Albert CISSELL (abt 1932 – 23 Nov 2012, CA)
   + Cody Elaine RUSSELL (1929 – 1992)
   + Madeline May SELLERS (14 Feb 1922 – 19 Aug 2012, CA)
  10 Edith Vava CISSELL (22 Nov 1933 – 2 Apr 2010, CA)
   + Joseph SABOL (abt 1933 Los Angeles, CA –)
    11 Steven J. SABOL (3 Jun 1958 Los Angeles, CA –)
    11 Lori Lynn SABOL (28 Oct 1959 Los Angeles, CA –)
     + Kevin A BERNET (1 Aug 1958 Bulawayo, Rhodesia –)
      12 Nicole Michelle BERNET (17 Jan 1988, CA –)
      12 Bradley Steven BERNET (28 Mar 1990, CA –)
    11 Donna Marie SABOL (20 Jun 1961 Los Angeles, CA –)
     + Timothy Richard GOLDSMITH
      12 Melissa Elaine GOLDSMITH (17 Feb 1993, CA –)
   + Donald Joseph DAVID (27 Aug 1925 – 21 Jan 1981, CA)
  10 William Lee CISSELL (12 Sep 1935, WA – 28 Mar 1974)
   + Harriet UKN1
    11 Rebecca CISSELL
  10 Norma Jean CISSELL (29 Jun 1937 – 3 Feb 2000, AZ)
   + George CHAVEZ (abt 29 May 1929 – abt 25 Aug 2000, NM)
    11 Kimberly CHAVEZ (5 Sep 1957 –)
     + Kurt KALBFLEISCH
      12 Heidi KALBFLEISCH
       + Andrew PEABODY
      12 Alanna KALBFLEISCH
     + Ukn GIBBONS
    11 Matthew L CHAVEZ (abt 31 Jul 1958 Belen, NM –)
     + Erin CHRISTIANSON
    11 Douglas F CHAVEZ (28 Jan 1959 Belen, NM –)
     + Sandra Lee SIMKO (abt 1962 –)
      12 CHAVEZ
    11 Derrick CHAVEZ (abt 8 Jun 1960 Belen, NM –)
     + Monica SMITH
      12 Daniel CHAVEZ (20 Mar 1987 Anaheim Hills, CA –)
       + Carina PALOMINA
      12 Michael CHAVEZ (12 Jan 1989 Anaheim Hills, CA –)
       + Candice UKN
        13 Levi CHAVEZ (abt Mar 2013 Ft. Collins, CO –)
    11 Brian Cissell CHAVEZ (8 Jun 1967 Belen, NM –)
     + Luzina Lynn ESTRADA (31 Aug 1966 –)
      12 Zachary CHAVEZ
      12 Joshua CHAVEZ
      12 Jacob CHAVEZ
      12 Maria CHAVEZ
      12 John-Paul CHAVEZ
      12 Simon CHAVEZ
      12 Gabriel CHAVEZ

9 Alice CISSELL (abt 1904 SD – 8 Jan 1906 Ponoka)
9 Harry Norman CISSELL (27 May 1907 – 27 Sep 1982, WA)
  + Ava SCOTT (abt 1917 – 3 Apr 1939 Yakima, WA)
   10 Ronald CISSELL (abt 1937 Yakima, WA –)
     + Peggy LEACH
      11 Susan CISSELL
     + Jeneveve WANNER
      11 Shaun Alexander Norman CISSELL
         + Ruby Lucille HAMMONTREE (abt 1959 –)
         12 Alexander CISSELL
         12 Tomas C. CISSELL (18 Jun 1990 –)
         + Christine Lea PAIGE (15 Oct 1964 –)
      + Virginia Lee (Plummer) WESTFALL
      + Marjorie L. LOWE
   10 Sharon L. CISSELL (1939 Yakima, WA –)
     + Larry Dewayne MAULDING (10 Apr 1938 – Dec 1989,WA)
      11 Larry Michael MAULDING (7 Aug 1957 San Diego, CA –)
         + Alice M GONZALEZ (abt 1950 –)
         12 Jennifer M MAULDING (abt 1987 –)
            + Derick WALKER
      11 Jerry MAULDING (11 Sep 1958 – 18 Nov 2009, CA)
     + Vincent FROEMEL (26 Aug 1934 – 22 May 2009, MN)
      11 Vincent Marshall FROEMEL (26 Oct 1970, CA –)
      11 Lori (Laura) Anne FROEMEL (9 Apr 1969, MN –)
         + Jeffery Allen SAMPLES
         + Mark MEISTER
         + Ukn
            12 Brookly Anne FROEMEL (8 Dec 1985 Ventura, CA –)
              + Paul Anthony RANGERE (7 Jul 1984 Ventura, CA –)
              + Jeremy LAHMANN
                13 Deegan Joseph LAHMANN (5 Sep 2010, CA –)
     + Geraldine Marie CALVIN (1920 – 28 Dec 2008 Oxnard, CA)
9 Vera (Pat) Chrystell CISSELL (5 Jul 1910 – 15 Oct 1972, WA)
  + Gilbert Edward GREDER (14 Sep 1910 – 25 Dec 1994, AZ)
9 Grace CISSELL (– d. inf.)
9 Clarence Arthur CISSELL (26 Aug 1913 – 8 May 1984, BC)
8 Etta M. (Hettie) CISSELL (abt 1869, MN – abt 1890)
  + W. F. "W. Frank" DAVIS
   9 Frank Daniels DAVIS (11 Mar 1890 SD – 19 Aug 1939, SD)
     + Sue (or Mary B) Ukn
      10 Emalyne M. DAVIS (19 Sep 1920 – 8 Mar 1992, WY)
        + Harvey William BROOKSMITH (abt 1918 – 10 Sep 1976)
         11 Harvey W. BROOKSMITH (17 Jun 1942 – 23 Aug 1985)
            + Susan UKN (1947 – 1988)
         11 Douglas J. BROOKSMITH (19 Jul 1949 – 31 Oct 1993)
            + Ukn
            12 Douglas J BROOKSMITH
         11 Terry BROOKSMITH
8 Julia CISSELL (abt 1871, MN – abt 1883 Ashland, MN)
8 Frank CISSELL (26 Sep 1873, MN – 15 May 1936 Ponoka)
  + Cora Emalyne WING (27 Mar 1876, Quebec – 3 Mar 1940)
   9 Florence May CISSELL (18 Mar 1895 – 10 Jan 1966 Ponoka)
     + Lynn Horatio MCCLAFLIN (16 Jan 1893 – 19 Sep 1953)

10 Wilfred MCCLAFLIN (Jul 1914 – Jul 1914 Ponoka)
10 Lawrence (Wilton) MCCLAFLIN (1 Jun 1915 –)
  + Irene WEBSTER
    11 Wade L. MCCLAFLIN (29 Jul 1952 –)
     + Candace SCOVORANSKI
      12 Cameron Lawrence RICE (1 Mar 1974 –)
       + Teresa MASON (19 Sep 1973 –)
        13 Cooper RICE (18 Aug 2000 –)
        13 Jared RICE (31 Oct 2001 –)
        13 Parker RICE (16 Jan 2004 –)
      12 Daniel Lawrence MCCLAFLIN (11 Mar 1981 –)
       + Tricia THOMSON (1 Jun 1981 –)
        13 Lillya Grace MCCLAFLIN (14 Jul 2011 –)
      12 Nathan William MCCLAFLIN (26 Mar 1985 –)
     + Kristiene WEBSTER (24 Dec 1954 –)
      12 Daniel Lawrence MCCLAFLIN (11 Mar 1981 –)
       + Tricia THOMSON (1 Jun 1981 –)
      12 Nathan William MCCLAFLIN (26 Mar 1985 –)
    11 Gerald Lynn MCCLAFLIN (19 Nov 1954 –)
     + Susan KASUR (15 Jul 1960 –)
    11 Clayton Del MCCLAFLIN (16 May 1956 –)
     + Diane ISSAC (31 Mar 1956 –)
      12 Brian MCCLAFLIN (25 Apr 1984 –)
      12 Charisse Audrey MCCLAFLIN (4 Feb 1986, AB –)
    11 Miles Lee MCCLAFLIN (17 Dec 1960 –)
     + Kimberly Jane ONESTO (22 Jan 1967 –)
      12 Colton MCCLAFLIN (16 Apr 1991 –)
      12 Destyn MCCLAFLIN (14 Jan 1994 –)
    11 Roxanne Lydia MCCLAFLIN (1 Apr 1963 –)
     + Leon ALGADZIS
      12 Elanta ALGADZIS (11 Feb 1995 –)
      12 Caleb ALGADZIS (24 Jul 1997 –)
    11 Lorne Ward MCCLAFLIN (23 Apr 1967 –)
     + Shirley SOMMER (2 Feb 1967 –)
      12 Zachary MCCLAFLIN (26 Feb 1990 –)
      12 Brandi Lynn MCCLAFLIN (25 Apr 1991 –)
      12 Kirk G. MCCLAFLIN (27 Nov 1992 – 22 May 1993)
      12 Katelyn MCCLAFLIN (21 Oct 1995 –)
      12 Lucas MCCLAFLIN (21 Oct 1995 – 21 Oct 1995)
    11 Twilla Joy MCCLAFLIN (11 Aug 1969 –)
     + Tbd TBD
      12 Tristan MCCLAFLIN (18 Feb 1987 –)
      12 Brenten MCCLAFLIN (15 Nov 1989 –)
10 Pearl Opal MCCLAFLIN (16 Jul 1916 – 1984)
  + Anthony "Tony" KESSLER (29 Dec 1916 – 29 Jun 1946)
    11 Noreen KESSLER (3 Sep 1938 –)
     + Gerald RYALL (4 Jun 1940 –)
      12 Jerry RYALL (10 May 1958 –)
      12 Janet RYALL (22 Nov 1959 –)
      12 Larry RYALL (8 Jan 1964 –)
      12 Terry RYALL (15 Feb 1965 –)
    11 Garry KESSLER (30 Dec 1939 – 1996)
    11 Esther KESSLER (20 Aug 1941 –)

+ Fred VAN ABS (25 Mar 1932 –)
  12 Kenny VAN ABS (21 Sep 1965 –)
  + Paige THOMPSON
  12 Lawrence VAN ABS (21 Sep 1965 –)
11 August KESSLER (12 Aug 1942 –)
+ Lil MONTIKA
  12 Tammy KESSLER (4 Jul 1976 –)
  12 Travis KESSLER (7 Nov 1981 –)
11 Orville Duane KESSLER (16 Jul 1943 –)
+ Sharon Fraser KESSLER (9 Jul 1945 –)
  12 Teresa Fay KESSLER (27 Sep 1966 –)
  + Scott BLOOMFIELD
    13 Lee Russell BLOOMFIELD (16 Oct 1986 –)
    13 Dean BLOOMFIELD (25 Jun 1989 –)
    13 Brett BLOOMFIELD (11 Jul 1992 –)
  + Duane GREEN (21 Mar 1960 –)
  12 Nancy May KESSLER (27 May 1969 –)
  + Mike MOCHID (27 Dec 1965 –)
    13 Jeff Michael MOCHID (28 Oct 1989 –)
    13 Steven Edward MOCHID (29 May 1991 –)
    13 Miranda May MOCHID (24 Nov 1994 –)
11 Faye Lottie KESSLER (11 Dec 1944, AB – 29 Jul 1963)
11 Juanita Betty KESSLER (16 Jun 1946 Calgary, AB –)
+ Donald Robert ALLEN (1 Oct 1946 –)
  12 Deborah Juanita ALLEN (6 Jan 1966 –)
  + Leon WIANCKO (11 Oct 1961 –)
    13 Ashley Juanita WIANCKO (18 Feb 1994 –)
    13 Alyssa Dawn WIANCKO (4 May 1999 –)
    13 Leanne Deborah WIANCKO (4 May 1999 –)
  12 Dwayne Donald ALLEN (27 May 1968 –)
  + Elaine Sarah EPP (3 Jun 1975 –)
    13 Monica Elaine ALLEN (10 Jan 2004 –)
+ William NAGEL (24 Aug 1910 –)
10 Leolla B. MCCLAFLIN (20 Apr 1920 – 17 Mar 1959 Ponoka)
+ Oswald JENSEN (15 Feb 1903 – 9 Apr 1972 Bashaw, AB)
11 Carl Lawrence JENSEN
+ Carol NEWTON
  12 Randy JENSEN (5 Apr 1967,AB –)
  + Maureen HALL
  + Trish MCPHEE (3 Oct 1966 –)
  12 Colleen JENSEN (12 Feb 1968 Ponoka, AB –)
  + Todd GADD (1 Jan 1968 –)
    13 Carlynn Brandi GADD (18 Jan 1991, AB –)
    + Joshua SOOKIAL
    13 Shayla Dusty GADD (13 May 1993 –)
  12 Jacqueline JENSEN (12 Nov 1968, AB –)
  + Darren PAULOVICH (4 Jul 1967 –)
    13 Braasen C. J. PAULOVICH (9 Jan 2002, AB –)
  12 Carmen JENSEN (13 Oct 1971 Ponoka –)
  + Gary TEBB (16 May 1969 –)
    13 Niklas Carsen TEBB (29 Aug 2002 –)
    13 Nathan Gary TEBB (28 Jan 2005 –)
  12 Janelle JENSEN (5 Jun 1979 –)

```
          + Clayton WEIGUM (2 Apr 1979 – )
            13 Charlese Sylvia WEIGUM (3 Feb 2005, AB – )
            13 Carl Jayce Clayton WEIGUM (11 Jun 2008, AB – )
            13 Bently Marcus WEIGUM (12 Sep 2011 Olds, AB – )
      11 Lynda May JENSEN
        + William TURNER
          12 Chris William TURNER (21 Jan 1970 – )
            + Kathy Lynn HOWARD (8 Aug 1973 – )
          12 Quintin Lee Turner TURNER (11 Mar 1971 – )
            + Lori FRASER (12 Jun 1970 – )
              13 Calvin Gerald TURNER (17 Jan 1997 – )
              13 Kimberly Leanne TURNER (29 Dec 1998 – )
          12 Kathryn Jean TURNER (13 Mar 1972 Ponoka, AB – )
            + Gary GEIGLE (13 Oct 1946 – )
      11 Janet Marie JENSEN (1 Jul 1958 Ponoka – )
        + Michael Ernest BARNES (1 Aug 1954 – )
          12 Mathew Zacariah BARNES (26 Jan 1981 – )
          + Roxanne FERREN
10 Audrey Violet MCCLAFLIN (6 Feb 1922 – 26 Mar 1990)
  + Chad WARNOCK (10 Jun 1922 – 3 Jun 1990)
10 Myrtle May MCCLAFLIN (10 May 1924 – 25 Feb 1982)
  + William Fredrick HILL (10 Jun 1922, SK – abt 2003)
    11 Deanna Muirene UKN (22 Sep 1943, AB – 22 Dec 2008)
      + Floyd Norman MCLEOD (30 Sep 1943 NB – )
        12 Floyd Norman Martin MCLEOD (29 Aug 1965 – )
          + Tbd TBD
            13 Floyd William Connar MCLEOD (4 Jul 1989 – )
            13 Callum MCLEOD (9 Oct 1995 – )
    11 Lana Belle HILL (29 Jan 1949 Calgary, AB – )
      + Dan MOWBRAY
        12 John William MOWBRAY (8 Jun 1966 – )
          + Tbd TBD
            13 Alicia MOWBRAY
      + Bruce WILSON
        12 Steven WILSON (21 Aug 1969, NB – )
        12 Kory Michael WILSON (7 Jul 1975, NB – )
        12 Dawn Marie WILSON (30 Nov 1977, NB – )
    11 Florence HILL (27 Mar 1953 Calgary, AB – )
      + Ukn TOOKE
        12 Kelly Jean TOOKE (8 Aug 1968 – )
      + Ukn FRASER
        12 Jody Mae FRASER (19 Feb 1976 – )
          + Ukn
            13 Jenna UKN
10 Walter Gordon MCCLAFLIN (7 Feb 1927 – )
  + Doreen Joy LUX (24 Jun 1927 – )
    11 Dwain Merl MCCLAFLIN (15 Jul 1951 – 12 Apr 2007)
    11 Diane Lynn MCCLAFLIN (26 Jan 1955 – )
      + John Forbes BROWN (22 Jan 1954 – )
        12 Cassandra Doreen BROWN (3 Aug 1982 – )
        12 Elissa Alexandra BROWN (18 Jul 1984 – )
        12 Rory Lynn Forbes BROWN (15 Jul 1986 – )
        12 Patrick John Walker BROWN (17 Mar 1988 – )
```

10 Thelma L. MCCLAFLIN (29 Oct 1929 – 12 Dec 1970, AB)
+ Kenneth Hartley RIDDIOUGH (12 Sep 1928 –)
11 Keith Hartley RIDDIOUGH (24 Jun 1954 –)
+ Barb BANNISTER (12 Dec 1957 – Jun 2012)
12 Shane Hartley RIDDIOUGH (5 May 1980 –)
+ (Name Unknown)
13 Kaida RIDDIOUGH (Dec 2005 –)
12 Kurt Andrew RIDDIOUGH (2 Jul 1983 –)
11 Kevin George RIDDIOUGH (15 Jun 1955 –)
+ Claire Louise RODE (15 Aug 1957 –)
12 Marcy RIDDIOUGH (30 Mar 1979 –)
+ Landon Nikirk TBD (20 Aug 1976 –)
13 Brett Landon RIDDIOUGH (3 Oct 2001 –)
13 Brody Dylan RIDDIOUGH (Apr 2003 –)
13 Dawson Ty RIDDIOUGH (24 Feb 2008 –)
12 Chantelle RIDDIOUGH (25 Dec 1980 –)
+ Unk BETTS
13 Dane Edward BETTS (31 Oct 2008 –)
12 Bradley Kevin RIDDIOUGH (10 Apr 1984 –)
+ (Name Unknown)
13 Dylan Rupert RIDDIOUGH (5 Jan 2009 –)
10 Infant MCCLAFLIN (1933 – 1933)
9 George Wing CISSELL (6 Sep 1896, SD – 11 Mar 1953, BC)
+ Alma May MCCULLOUGH (27 May 1901 – 11 Mar 1984)
10 George Glenn CISSELL (6 Nov 1922 –)
+ Cynthia Doreem BERTRAM (25 Nov 1929 – 9 Apr 2005)
11 Cynthia Doreen CISSELL (13 Mar 1958, Haney, BC –)
+ (Name Unknown)
12 Michael UKN (25 Apr 1982 –)
12 Ryan UKN (3 May 1983 –)
11 Raymond Glenn CISSELL (7 Jan 1964, BC –)
+ (Name Unknown)
12 Samantha CISSELL (14 Sep 1994 –)
+ (Name Unknown)
13 Ukn
12 Dyllan CISSELL (9 Dec 1998 –)
11 Keith Wayne CISSELL (11 Oct 1964 Haney, BC –)
+ Nicole PINCHUCK (1973 –)
12 Christian CISSELL (14 Mar 1990 –)
12 Derrick CISSELL
11 David George CISSELL (2 Oct 1967, Edmonton –)
+ Marti YAKUBOW
12 Amber CISSELL (28 Apr 1988 –)
+ (Name Unknown)
13 Ty David UKN (21 Dec 2011 –)
12 Jodi CISSELL (11 Dec 1990 –)
+ (Name Unknown)
13 Lian John UKN (6 May 2009 –)
13 Myah UKN (abt Sep 2012 –)
12 Torrie CISSELL (20 Feb 1994 –)
12 Devon CISSELL (bef 2000 –)
+ (Name Unknown)
12 Tristan Cynthia CISSELL (11 Nov 1995 –)

10 Alma Marguerite CISSELL (5 Jun 1925 Ponoka, AB – 1961)
+ Arthur LEMKE (25 Apr 1918 – 16 Feb 2002)
    11 Leslie Robert LEMKE (18 Jun 1943 –)
        + Eileen MCHUGH
            12 Belinda McHugh LEMKE (21 Mar 1976 –)
                + Bill LAUZON
                + Charles Thomas KROCHAK
                    13 Tanner Evan KROCHAK (16 Aug 2011 –)
    11 Vincent Duane LEMKE (31 Jan 1946 –)
        + Ruth CHARTERS (11 May 1947 –)
            12 Dana Ruth LEMKE (20 Dec 1971 Kimberley, BC –)
                + Steven HALLER
                    13 Kyran Rose HALLER (21 Jun 1998 –)
                    13 Abigail Lynn HALLER (22 Nov 1999 –)
                    13 Marrin Karoline HALLER (20 Dec 2001 –)
            12 Duane Vincent LEMKE (15 Jan 1973 BC –)
                + Anita KORCORAN
                    13 Kala Skye LEMKE (8 Apr 2004 –)
                    13 Karissa Page LEMKE (5 Jul 2007 –)
    11 Douglas LEMKE (27 Dec 1950 Ponoka –)
        + Margaret CATHRO (21 Jan 1951 –)
            12 Shaun LEMKE (15 Feb 1974 –)
                + Sarah GLOVER
                    13 Gabriella Reed LEMKE (24 Apr 2006 –)
                    13 Connor Arthur LEMKE (15 Nov 2010 –)
            12 Cory LEMKE (Nov 1976 –)
                + Jodi TOMCHYSHYN
                + Chelsa GONDEK
                    13 Declan Jude LEMKE (23 May 2012 –)
    11 Beverly LEMKE (7 Nov 1952 –)
        + Clifford BUNNY (10 Aug 1947 –)
            12 Laurie BUNNY (17 Apr 1970 –)
            12 Nicole BUNNY (9 Aug 1972 Whitecourt, AB –)
                + Jason Lee BATIUK (24 Oct 1978 –)
                    13 Isadora Elizabeth BATIUK (6 Jul 2010 –)
                    13 Lucas James BATIUK (21 Aug 2012 –)
            12 Shane BUNNY (5 Jan 1976 –)
    11 Kevin LEMKE (20 Nov 1957 Ponoka, Alberta, Canada –)
        + Suzanne SMID
9 Raymond C. CISSELL (abt Aug 1903 Ponoka – 26 Dec 1905)
9 Lodema Thelma CISSELL (5 Sep 1905 Ponoka – 29 Mar 2004)
+ Loring MARSH
    10 Opal Viaolla MARSH (18 Oct 1924 Ponoka, AB –)
        + STEWART
            11 Stanley STEWART (18 Jun 1945 –)
            11 Diane STEWART (20 Jul 1946 –)
            11 Larry STEWART (1948 –)
        + Kenneth CUNNINGHAM
            11 Donald CUNNINGHAM
            11 Tommy CUNNINGHAM
            11 Sharon CUNNINGHAM
        + Ronald THORNE
+ Ernest Dewey (Pete) ALLISON (8 Jan 1908 – 20 Dec 1983)

10 Carrie Emeline ALLISON (6 Dec 1931 Rimbey, AB –)
+ Ignace Frank FREY (12 Oct 1927 Hungary –)
  11 Shirley Ann FREY (8 May 1952 Oliver, BC –)
  + Harold FLECK (4 Mar 1948 –)
    12 Annette Christine FLECK (15 Jun 1971 Calgary –)
    + Jason Richard SPALDING (11 Feb 1970 –)
    12 Karen Ann Marie FLECK (26 May 1973 Calgary –)
    + David BAILLIE
      13 Nathan BAILLIE (9 Dec 2010 –)
  11 Joseph Ernest FREY (4 Nov 1953 Oliver, BC –)
  + Sue Ann Jessie BALES (25 Sep 1956 –)
    12 Shawna Lynn FREY (20 Jan 1978 –)
    12 Kenneth Frank FREY (19 Aug 1979 –)
  11 Richard Frank FREY (7 Feb 1955 Oliver, BC –)
  + Susan Dorothy KOZUB (2 Jan 1956 – 8 Feb 1997)
  + Sandra Lee OSBORNE (4 Jun 1961 –)
    12 Natalie Janeil FREY (15 May 1990 –)
  11 Sandra Kaye FREY (17 Oct 1956 Ponoka, AB –)
  + David DUBBIN (25 May 1956 –)
    12 David Ernest DUBBIN (24 Mar 1985 –)
    12 Jason Frank DUBBIN (21 Feb 1988 –)
  11 Donald George FREY (2 Sep 1959 Calgary, AB –)
  + Jocelyn UKN (19 Jul 1960 –)
    12 Kaitlynn Avonne FREY (23 Jul 1992 –)
    12 Camille Paige FREY (25 May 1995 –)
10 Gertrude Lodema ALLISON (23 Jul 1936 Ponoka, AB –)
+ Joseph L. PREFONTAINE (22 Mar 1936 – 4 Aug 2010)
  11 Edward Charles PREFONTAINE (5 May 1957 Calgary –)
  + Marilyn Elaine OLSEN (24 Jun 1958 – 13 Jun 1977)
  11 Patrick Ernest PREFONTAINE (6 Aug 1958 Calgary –)
  + Andrea Joyce CONSTABLE (22 Sep 1961 –)
    12 Matthew William PREFONTAINE (15 Dec 1992 –)
    12 Mariea Nicole PREFONTAINE (15 Aug 1994 –)
    12 Kathryn Elizabeth PREFONTAINE (8 Dec 1997 –)
  11 James A. PREFONTAINE (19 Sep 1959 – 11 Jan 1978)
  11 Carolyn Thelma M. PREFONTAINE (20 Sep 1960 –)
  + Brian MALLEY
    12 Jennifer MALLEY (1 Apr 1977 –)
    + Brian Wayne MCLELLAN (19 Aug 1970 –)
      13 Joshua Robert MCLELLAN (8 Apr 2002 –)
      13 Kristin Jade MCLELLAN (12 Jul 2005 –)
      13 Liam Joseph MCLELLAN (4 Jan 2008 –)
  + Derik LANE
    12 Kyle James Alexander LANE (13 Mar 1983 –)
    + Tanya Nicole MASON (9 Mar 1984 –)
      13 Erek Alexander LANE (29 Oct 2001 –)
      13 Kaden LANE
    12 Jamie Michael LANE (18 Jun 1984 –)
  + Robert Murray DIXON (2 Dec 1956 –)
  11 David Lawrence PREFONTAINE (16 Mar 1966 AB –)
  + Natalie Ann SAUNDERS (22 Mar 1967 –)
    12 Jessica Michele PREFONTAINE (9 Jun 2001 –)
  11 Faye Marie PREFONTAINE (5 Apr 1968 –)

+ Shawn Michael CRAVEN (16 Jun 1967 –)
  12 Allison Jeanette CRAVEN (29 Aug 1995 –)
  12 Erica Rose CRAVEN (23 Aug 1998 –)
10 George Dale ALLISON (23 May 1937 –)
+ Margaret Anne EVANS (9 Jun 1968 –)
9 Emma Lottie CISSELL (17 Feb 1910 – 18 Apr 2012 Ponoka)
+ Milton Rockwell OLMSTEAD (9 Nov 1904 – 6 Sep 1977)
10 Inez Louise OLMSTEAD (11 Oct 1935 – 1 Nov 1993)
+ Ronald Percy DOUPE (17 Jun 1929 – 23 Mar 2007)
  11 Ronald Lynn DOUPE (3 Oct 1957 –)
  + Kim GORE (28 Aug 1957 –)
  12 Chelsea Dawn DOUPE (6 Aug 1986 –)
  12 Breane Louise DOUPE (30 Jun 1988 –)
  11 Edwin Wesley DOUPE (26 Oct 1959 –)
  + Lise RUNITE (24 Mar 1959 –)
  12 Evan Marshall DOUPE (29 Dec 1987 –)
  12 Branden Tyler DOUPE (30 Oct 1991 –)
  12 Lauryn Candice DOUPE (15 Sep 1993 –)
  11 Pearl Louise DOUPE (19 Jun 1961 –)
  11 Trent Ernest DOUPE (28 May 1964 –)
  + Joanne Caroline HENKELMAN (14 Jul 1963 –)
  12 Sam Milton DOUPE (8 Jan 1994 –)
  12 Louise Caroline DOUPE (24 Aug 1995 –)
10 Kenneth Darrell OLMSTEAD (15 Dec 1938 – 13 Sep 2010)
+ Donna Gayle PHILLIPS
+ Leona (Fluet) IRVINE (3 Sep 1936 – 23 Jul 1998)
10 Donna Marie OLMSTEAD (21 Feb 1948 –)
+ Richard Nicolas STREET (19 Apr 1946 –)
  11 Sandra Marie STREET (25 Sep 1968 Ponoka, AB –)
  + Douglas Owen John LUND (3 Dec 1958 –)
  12 Alexandria Marie LUND (13 Jan 1997 –)
  11 Katherine Rose STREET (29 Jul 1970 Ponoka, AB –)
  + Bradley OLSEN (3 Aug 1965 –)
  12 Steven Bradley OLSEN (18 Sep 1997 –)
  12 Emma Rose OLSEN (12 Apr 2004 –)
9 Walter Merl CISSELL (13 Aug 1914 Ponoka – 13 Mar 1984)
+ Hilda Irma MASS (1 Mar 1921 – 23 Jul 2009)
10 Judy May CISSELL (24 Feb 1943 Ponoka, AB –)
+ Jerry Raymond MILLER (21 Aug 1942 – 10 Sep 1996)
  11 Mark Gregory MILLER (8 Aug 1972 Ponoka, AB –)
  + Pamela Dawn ANDERSON (12 Nov 1974 –)
  11 Gregory Mark MILLER (14 Jul 1974 –)
  + Jolene Nicole LARSON (25 Feb 1974 –)
  12 Nate Micah MILLER (25 Nov 2007 –)
  12 Neriah May MILLER (17 Jul 2009 –)
+ Merle Lee JONES (10 Aug 1939 –)
10 Elaine Ann CISSELL (1 Aug 1945 Ponoka, AB –)
+ Richard Alfred GROOM (1 Mar 1945 –)
  11 Monica Elaine GROOM (14 Jul 1969 Red Deer, AB –)
  + Jeffery James HARVEY (28 Nov 1969 –)
  12 Jonah Lewis HARVEY (27 Oct 1995 –)
  12 Virginia Lane HARVEY (1 May 1997 –)
  12 Julianna Grace HARVEY (29 Mar 2000 –)

        11 Ronald Richard GROOM (15 Apr 1972 – 14 Nov 1998)
      10 Frank David CISSELL (19 Apr 1947 –)
       + Patricia Anne PALECHEK (15 Feb 1946 –)
        11 Chad David CISSELL (29 Sep 1969 –)
         + Alana JOHNSON (8 Jul 1969 –)
          12 Erika Ann CISSELL (26 Oct 1994 –)
          12 Brett Charles CISSELL (21 Dec 1997 –)
        11 Chantelle Patricia CISSELL (4 May 1972 –)
         + Darren GODFREY (29 Jun 1969 –)
          12 Logan Chistopher GODFREY (7 May 2003 –)
          12 Jordan Emily GODFREY (2 Mar 2005 –)
      10 Connie Cora CISSELL (31 May 1953 –)
       + Bryan Ross PRETULA (18 Nov 1953 –)
        11 Leanne Connie PRETULA (1 Aug 1977 –)
        11 Steven Bryan PRETULA (6 Nov 1981 –)
         + Crystal Marie DEROUIN (1 Mar 1981 –)
          12 John Louis PRETULA (12 Dec 2010 –)
          12 Paisley Marie PRETULA (10 Dec 2012 –)
    9 (Baby) CISSELL (abt 1916 Ponoka, Alberta, Canada – abt 1916)
8 Alice L. CISSELL (1 Jun 1875, MN – 29 Mar 1901, SD)
 + Richard J. MUELLER (5 Jul 1861 WI – 22 Sep 1958, SD)
8 Willie CISSELL (21 Oct 1877– 19 Nov 1878 Ashland, MN)
8 Mary CISSELL (18 Jan 1880, MN – 20 Jan 1881 Ashland, MN)
8 Emma Rose CISSELL (abt 25 Aug 1883 – 30 Aug 1950 Volga, SD)
 + Emil Marius WOLD (22 Jun 1878 Norway – 3 Apr 1945)
 + Edward B. KENLY (Nov 1887 MN – 3 Jan 1940 Volga, SD)
 + Hans C. KALBERG (26 Apr 1879 SD – 1 Mar 1948, SD)
8 Bessie (Carrie) May CISSELL (Apr 1885 – 18 Feb 1947 Yakima)
 + Clinton Dewitt BAILEY (Nov 1873 –)
  9 Minerva BAILEY (13 Nov 1904 Ponoka – 12 Nov 1969 Yakima)
   + John Manly HULL (5 May 1899, IA – 24 Mar 1982 Toppenish)
    10 Glenn Arthur HULL (25 Feb 1922 – 30 Aug 2010 WA)
     + Elaine Helen CARL (16 Feb 1924 – 17 Apr 1985 Yakima)
      11 Ronald HULL (8 Sep 1944 – abt 1975)
       + Ukn
        12 Clay Martin HULL (8 Aug 1971 –)
       + (Name Unknown)
      11 Carl Francis HULL (8 Jul 1942 – 15 Aug 2008 OR)
       + Arlene L MERCY
        12 Brian C HULL (11 Feb 1966 –)
         + Jennifer J. MERCY (10 May 1976 –)
          13 Child 1 HULL
          13 Child 2 HULL
          13 Child 3 HULL
      11 Joyce HULL (abt 1945 WA – 5 Aug 1945 Yakima)
      11 Stephen Alan HULL (13 Sep 1946 –)
       + Paula Josephine DUFAULT (1 Nov 1946 –)
        12 Alaina M. HULL (15 Feb 1986 –)
      11 Joseph HULL
     + Barbara SWANSON (15 Sep 1932 –)
    10 Lorraine A. HULL (12 Sep 1924 – 26 Jun 2008 Yakima, WA)
     + Lloyd "Bud" SYLLING (8 Mar 1922 ND – 16 Apr 2002 WA)
      11 Phyllis SYLLING (11 Feb 1944 Wapato, WA –)

+ Michael D. MILLER (10 Dec 1940 –)
  12 Timothy Michael MILLER (21 Jul 1962 –)
11 Jean Marie SYLLING (29 Jun 1947 – 29 Jun 1947)
11 Johnny Lloyd SYLLING (Jun 1949 – 31 Mar 2013, WA)
  + Ukn
    12 Johnny Lloyd Jr. SYLLING (abt 1970 –)
      + Katie Ivey UKN (abt 1978 –)
        13 Grace SYLLING
        13 Warren SYLLING
    12 Stace (Jim Cline) SYLLING
    12 Linda HALE
    12 Sarah Lee HALE
      + Blake OURSO
        13 Haylee OURSO
    12 Phillip W. HALE (1 Mar 1975 –)
11 Bobbi Ray SYLLING (27 Jun 1954 Yakima, WA –)
  + Mike A. GILLESPIE (7 Sep 1953 –)
    12 Jason Allen GILLESPIE (15 Jun 1981 –)
      + Cara WATTS
    12 Ryan James GILLESPIE (9 Feb 1985 –)
      + Whitney PILZ (2 Jul 1982 –)
11 Rebecca "Becky" SYLLING (27 Jun 1954 Yakima, WA –)
  + Oscar Charles FINLEY
    12 Oscar Charles Jr. FINLEY (5 Sep 1976 –)
    12 Brian FINLEY (5 Apr 1982 –)
+ Harold Emmett MITCHELL (1903 – 3 Feb 1950 Yakima, WA)
+ Clifford Wesley HYDE (– 13 Aug 1955 Yakima, WA)
+ Ukn MCTEER
9 Ada BAILEY (Dec 1908 Ponoka – 15 Dec 1982 Spokane, WA)
+ Hershel MCNAIR (28 Oct 1902 – 25 Feb 1973 Entait, WA)
  10 Dennis MCNAIR (1 Nov 1948 –)
  + Judith Marie LAWSON
    11 Shawn MCNAIR (1967 Yakima, WA –)
  + Diana K. SPRUELL (17 Mar 1955 –)
    11 Tara MCNAIR (1977 –)
      + Ukn SHAFFER
        12 Preston SHAFFER (10 Dec 1993 –)
      + Ukn HAMMER
        12 Kailyn HAMMER (29 Sep 1997 –)
    11 Shane Robert MCNAIR (6 Aug 1979 –)
      + Jenn STOKES
        12 Britany Marie MCNAIR (28 Jun 1999 –)
  + Linda MCCART
    11 Tawnya MCNAIR
      + Ukn JORDON
        12 Paige JORDON
        12 Hayden JORDON
        12 Ethan JORDON
    11 Brent MCNAIR (abt 1974 –)
  + Sue KISSINGER
  + Dorothy ALDIN
  + Kathleen L. KISH (2 Aug 1951 –)
    11 Tara MCNAIR (abt 1977 –)

```
          + Ukn SHAFFER
            12 Preston SHAFFER
            12 Jonathan M. SHAFFER
       + Alvin Earl CHAMBERLAIN
         10 Gerald Alvin CHAMBERLAIN (18 Apr 1928 – )
         + Ukn WISSINK
         10 Beverly Mona CHAMBERLAIN (13 Jul 1929 Yakima – )
           + Victor SINNOTT (abt 1921, MN – 22 Dec 1999 Spokane)
             11 Jerri SINNOTT (abt 1950 – )
             + Tbd GROH
             11 Ron SINNOTT (9 Aug 1954 poss. in Spokane, WA – )
             11 Sharon M. SINNOTT (3 Apr 1958 – )
               + Terry N. PIERCE (11 Nov 1947 – )
                 12 Lindsey PIERCE (31 Aug 1986 – )
             11 Donna SINNOTT
  9  Melvin Everett BAILEY (20 May 1911 – 29 May 1996, WA)
    + Florence WOODARD
    + Annabelle Z. ZIMMERMAN (10 Jan 1922 – 10 Sep 2009, WA)
      10 Connie G. BAILEY (1940 – )
        + Gerald L. TALLMADGE (1941 – )
      10 Bonnie BAILEY (13 Jun 1941 – )
        + John E. BUCHOLTZ (8 Mar 1937 – )
      10 Donna BAILEY (abt 1943 – 1981)
      10 Melvin Frederick BAILEY (1948 – )
        + Linda Mae SIMONSON
          11 Darrin Everitt BAILEY (18 May 1971 – )
            + (Name Unknown)
            12 Unk BAILEY
          11 Andrea Doreen BAILEY (23 Oct 1972 – )
           + John Glen BLANCHARD (14 Nov 1959 – )
             12 Michael John BLANCHARD (26 Oct 1991 – )
             12 Taylor BLANCHARD (abt 1995 – )
      10 Janet BAILEY (25 Mar 1951 – )
        + Gary A MATTHIESEN (15 Sep 1948 – )
          11 Bradley J. MATTHIESEN (1981 – )
          11 Megan Marie MATTHIESEN (14 Jul 1983 Vancouver – )
          + Joshua Robert ROBSON (20 Jun 1981 – )
  9 Alice (Elsie) BAILEY (16 Jan 1914 Ponoka – 30 May 1981 OR)
    + Viril Lloyd GARRISON
      10 Donald Dean GARRISON (25 Sep 1932 – 20 Nov 1991, OR)
        + Bethine Vonita FETTERS (1936 NE – )
          11 Dale Alan GARRISON (12 Jul 1955 – )
            + Donna Marie HALL (abt 1956 – )
              12 David Vonley GARRISON (23 Sep 1974 – )
                + Meadow DORNE
                  13 Anthea Datura GARRISON (23 Jan 2005 – )
                  13 Bailin Rain GARRISON (20 Sep 2008 – )
              12 Daniel James GARRISON (24 Jan 1976 – )
                + Abigail Marie ZAROSINSKI (25 Aug 1986 – )
                  13 Henry Dean GARRISON (24 Jan 2013 – )
              12 Douglas Dean GARRISON (24 Jan 1978 – )
                + Laura N. BAILEY (10 Mar 1977 – )
                  13 Declan James GARRISON (25 Apr 2012 – )
```

11 Don Robert GARRISON (31 May 1957 –)
+ Angle BECK (24 Apr 1958 –)
+ Cheryl Lynn WEBB
11 Debra Lynn GARRISON (25 Jul 1959 –)
+ David BARRERA (13 Aug 1957 –)
12 Deann Bethine BARRERA (12 Jul 1978 –)
+ Tim CAIN
12 Aric BARRERA (24 Aug 1979 –)
+ Brenda Kaye BEYER (22 Nov 1979 –)
13 Emma Lauren BARRERA (22 Nov 2003 –)
13 Cole David BARRERA (5 Jul 2005 –)
13 Olivia Morgan BARRERA (4 Nov 2008 –)
13 Kourtney Paige BARRERA (8 Sep 2010 –)
12 Jared Elias BARRERA (9 Dec 1980 –)
+ Tanya ADAMS (12 Dec 1980 –)
13 Caitlin BARRERA (16 Jul 2004 –)
13 Jackson Jared BARRERA (21 May 2007 –)
13 Carson David BARRERA (15 Jan 2009 –)
13 Aslin BARRERA (18 Aug 2012 –)
12 Aaron Sixto BARRERA (7 Feb 1983 –)
+ James P VAN ATTA (abt 1905 – 11 Jun 1945, Yakima, WA)
+ John P. MATTOX
10 Scott Vaughn MATTOX (25 Dec 1947 Yakima, WA –)
+ Diane Marie UKN (1 Oct 1949 Eureka, IL –)
11 Anne Marie MATTOX (abt 1981 –)
+ Ian PARKS
12 Elsie PARKS (abt Jan 2013 Portland, OR –)
11 David Michael MATTOX (abt 1983 –)
+ Davina MENDIBURU
+ Walter W. DAVIS (abt 1886 MA –)
7 Mary Ann CISSELL (25 Jan 1844, MO – 11 Apr 1909 Perry Co, MO)
+ Feriol PREVALLET
8 Albert M PREVALLET (1 May 1866 – abt 1911)
8 Mary Louise PREVALLET (22 Sep 1869 – 28 Feb 1907)
8 Mary Genevieve PREVALLET (7 Jan 1872 – 17 Oct 1929)
8 William Joseph PREVALLET (15 May 1874 –)
8 Mary Henrietta PREVALLET (30 Dec 1876 – 11 Apr 1912)
8 Mary Anna PREVALLET (1 Jul 1882 – abt 1929)
7 Lewis Clark CISSELL (11 Nov 1847, MO – 14 Apr 1923 Perry Co, MO)
+ Anna VESSELLS
8 Emmett CISSELL (1 Sep 1873 –)
8 Thomas Edwin CISSELL (22 Feb 1875 – 19 Sep 1948)
8 Charles Arthur CISSELL (10 Oct 1877 – 5 May 1910)
8 John Maurice CISSELL (9 Dec 1879 – 4 Jan 1954)
8 Joseph Elliot CISSELL (7 Aug 1884 – 17 Jun 1950)
8 Mary Olivia CISSELL (2 Oct 1886 – abt 1956)
8 Francis Lee CISSELL (16 Jan 1889 – 13 Jan 1956)
8 George CISSELL (24 Jun 1893 – bef 1928)
8 Unk CISSELL (– bef 1928)
8 Nerius Lonnie CISSELL (6 Feb 1895 – Nov 1982)
7 Thomas CISSELL (4 Oct 1849 Perry Co, MO – abt 1870)
7 Julia CISSELL (17 Jan 1852 Perry Co, MO – 3 Jun 1928 Perryville, MO)
+ Maurice (Moritz) PREVALLET

    8 Mary PREVALLET (4 Sep 1872 –)
    8 Ann Abella PREVALLET (16 May 1874 –)
    8 Joseph PREVALLET (22 Feb 1876 –)
    8 Thomas Elmore PREVALLET (11 Dec 1879 – abt 1928)
    8 John Leonard PREVALLET (2 Jan 1884 – 23 Feb 1950)
    8 Minnie PREVALLET (– abt 1950)
    8 Ernest M. PREVALLET (14 Jun 1890 – 6 Dec 1945)
  7 Peter C. CISSELL (9 Sep 1855 Perry Co, MO –)
   + America BURGEE
    8 Elizabeth Marie CISSELL (1879 –)
    8 Birdie CISSELL
    8 Julie CISSELL
    8 Clarence CISSELL
    8 Herman CISSELL
    8 Ella CISSELL
    8 Corine CISSELL
    8 Grace CISSELL
  7 Mary Caroline CISSELL (13 Dec 1862 Perry Co, MO –)
  7 Robert Joseph CISSELL (23 Feb 1869 Perry Co, MO –)
  7 Charles Joseph CISSELL (25 Aug 1872 Perry Co, MO –)
 + Julia BROWN
6 Vincent CISSELL (15 Oct 1821, MO – 20 Mar 1903 Perry Co, MO)
 + Mary Caroline FRENCH
  7 Leo Ferdinand CISSELL (1847 – 1851)
  7 Mary Lavinia CISSELL (16 Aug 1848 – 21 May 1922)
  7 Victoria Anna CISSELL (9 Aug 1851 – 17 Feb 1925)
  7 Mary Ann CISSELL (16 Sep 1853 – 10 Nov 1918)
  7 Celestian Albert CISSELL (1 Oct 1857 – 29 Jan 1927)
  7 Anna Ambrosia CISSELL (3 Mar 1860 – 25 May 1965)
6 Lewis CISSELL (20 Jul 1823 Perry Co, MO – 13 Apr 1892 St. Mary, MO)
 + Louisa Jane MATTINGLY
  7 John Verius(Veris) CISSELL (abt 17 Aug 1847 – 9 Dec 1891)
  7 Ann Loretta CISSELL (4 Jan 1849 –)
  7 Leo Ferdinand CISSELL (7 Mar 1852 – 23 Nov 1901)
  7 Mary Teresa CISSELL (2 Oct 1853 – 12 Mar 1867)
  7 Joseph Emmanuel CISSELL (12 Apr 1856 – 11 Jan 1916)
  7 Ezekiel CISSELL (11 May 1857 – 19 Jan 1893)
  7 Mary Jane Francis CISSELL (12 Jun 1859 – 2 Feb 1939)
  7 Lewis Kenrick(Kendrick) CISSELL (24 Feb 1861 – 23 Oct 1928)
  7 Henry Pius CISSELL (16 Dec 1862 – Mar 1867)
  7 Mary Louisa CISSELL (30 Apr 1865 – Nov 1865)
  7 Vincent CISSELL (3 Feb 1868 – 12 Dec 1942)
  7 William Aloysius CISSELL (23 Jan 1870 – 1939)
6 Henry Pius CISSELL (31 Mar 1825, MO – 10 Jan 1877 Perry Co, MO)
 + Christina MILES
  7 Mary Anastasia CISSELL (30 Jan 1851 – 1 Aug 1921)
  7 Vincent CISSELL (3 Sep 1852 –)
  7 Joseph Francis CISSELL (1 Sep 1854 – 20 Mar 1877)
  7 John Arcinius CISSELL (abt 24 Dec 1856 – bur. 20 Oct 1865)
  7 Mary Christina CISSELL (29 Dec 1858 – 1921)
  7 Francis Xavier CISSELL (9 Nov 1860 – 20 Mar 1877)
  7 Henry Pius Jr. CISSELL (27 Apr 1863 –)
6 Leo CISSELL (10 Apr 1836 Perry Co, MO – 4 Mar 1842 Perry Co, MO)

      6 Henry Angelo CISSELL (Jul 1838, MO – 27 Dec 1838 Perry Co, MO)
      6 Joseph Clement CISSELL (15 Apr 1840, MO – 19 Sep 1872 Perry Co, MO)
        + Rosalie Philomena DUVALL
          7 Henry Leo CISSELL (6 Nov 1866 – 2 Sep 1872)
          7 Edwina Maria CISSELL (bap. 26 Jan 1868 –)
          7 John Leonard CISSELL (26 Jan 1870 –)
          7 James Matthew (Maddison) CISSELL (12 Feb 1872 – 19 Aug 1937)
      6 Leo CISSELL (14 May 1842 Perry Co, MO – 25 Nov 1861 Perry Co, MO)
      6 Mary Ann CISSELL (abt 1845, MO – 11 Mar 1922 Perryville, MO)
        + Simon Sylvester TUCKER
      6 Julia CISSELL (abt 1852 Perry Co, MO –)
     + Mary (Manning) WARREN
   4 Susanna CISSELL (28 Jan 1760 St. Mary's Co, MD –)
   4 Peter CISSELL (29 Jan 1764 – abt 1803 Washington Co, KY)
   4 Rachael CISSELL
   4 Annastatia CISSELL
   4 Rebecca CISSELL
   4 James Rodney CISSELL (8 Apr 1762 St. Mary's Co, MD –)
3 Mary CISSELL
3 Ruth CISSELL

Overall Family Tree

Selected Index

Note: To the extent possible, women are listed by their maiden names.

It's sweet to be remembered
By loved ones far away
Whose days are filled with busy hours
Though thoughts will sometimes stray
To others who still love one, though
They seldom write to tell one so
For as the years go swiftly by
They older grow apace
And Father Time with beckoning hand
Soon bids one go with grace.

Anna Holden King
to
Lois Holden Cissell
1949

Corrections

In preparing this book, representatives from each of the main family branches were asked for information on their branches. Some provided that information; some did not know about all of their family members; and some did not reply. Accordingly, some errors and omissions should be expected.

Space to record any needed changes are provided on the following pages.

Corrections and additions may also be reported by email to yakimacissells@gmail.com and would be appreciated[261].

---

[261] At least through 2018, the 360th year of the family in North America.

Corrections

Page	Changes or Additions

Page	Changes or Additions

Page	Changes or Additions

Page	Changes or Additions

Page	Changes or Additions

Page	Changes or Additions

конец

www.ingramcontent.com/pod-product-compliance
Lightning Source LLC
Chambersburg PA
CBHW081822280526
45789CB00007B/2300